MONEY
Still
NUMBER
ONE

The Single Man's *Survival* Guide to
Thailand

By
Neil Hutchison

Published and Distributed by:
Mitraphab Centre Pty Ltd
Tumbi Umbi, NSW 2261
AUSTRALIA

Illustrations by:
Khun Porn
Metal Tattoo & Art
Pattaya, Thailand

Cover Design by:
Neil Hutchison

Written by:
Neil Hutchison
Email: hutcho_ph@hotmail.com

ISBN: 0-9751349-4-9

Other Titles

Money Number One
The Single Man's Survival Guide to Pattaya
First Released: 25 December 2001
(Out of print. Superceded by this edition.)

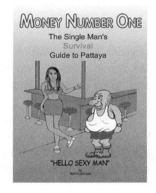

A Fool in Paradise
First Released: 22 November 2003

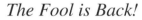

The Fool is Back!
First Released: 1 November 2004

Acknowledgements

Special thanks to my good friend, Frank Lauerbach, who I hold personally responsible for introducing me to the delights of Pattaya. Whatever mess I found myself in, he was always there to tell me what I should have done. Thanks, Frank.

My eternal gratitude must go to Alan McEwan for his faith, encouragement and support. Alan offered many suggestions and contributed tales from his own experience for inclusion in this book. Gratifying to know not all the screw-ups are mine.

Thanks also to Duncan Stearn whose input and constructive criticism was very much appreciated.

Last, but definitely not least, thank you to all the people who sent me e-mails after reading *Money Number One*. Your encouraging comments and support made my efforts and expensive research all worthwhile. Please keep them coming.

Disclaimer

You can not write a book like this without shirking all responsibility for the content. So, here goes:

This book is a generalization that contains anecdotes and references to personal experiences, observations and opinions. Stories relating to personal experiences are as accurate as my alcohol-abused brain will allow. Absolutely no effort has been made to check the authenticity of the stories told to me by third parties. Stories passed on by word of mouth tend to change somewhat each time they are related, but I have included them because, in my opinion, each one reflects a very plausible scenario. Any similarity or resemblance to any person alive or dead is their problem.

If you come to Thailand for a holiday, follow my tips and advice and still fuck up, it's your problem.

The prices referred to throughout this book are quoted in Thai *Baht*. They are approximate and should only be used as a guide.

Contents

Introduction

*"It may be that your sole purpose in life is
simply to serve as a warning to others."*

Anyone wanting to read about Thai history, arts and crafts, the temples, the scenery or the beaches, do not read on. Buy a book from one of the many bookshops or tourist agencies. If you want to know about the shopping, the markets, the best hotels, the restaurants or the many tourist attractions then again, this book is not for you. This book is for the pure pleasure seeker, the male hedonist. It is meant for those millions of male tourists who descend on Thailand each year. Coming from freezing temperatures in their home countries, filled with equally cold females, it can be quite a shock to the system.

Money Number One, released on Christmas Eve 2001, was designed to help first-timers navigate through the tricks and quirks of Pattaya's lifestyle as well as give Thailand veterans something to chuckle over. The response from readers was overwhelming. Although it was impossible to cover every contingency, from the feedback received to date, what the book did cover has not been challenged.

Of all the comments I received about *Money Number One*, three in particular kept recurring. The first was obvious:

"I wish I had read this book before I first set foot in Thailand." Me too. The book attempted to explain many of the traps that abound for the men who arrive here to discover that a thirst is mandatory, a fat wallet is obligatory and morality is listed as an optional extra.

The newly arrived male visitor finds himself in a Disneyland for adults, a place unlike anywhere else on this planet. He sees the neon Pattaya that greets the holidaymaker, wears him down, chews him up then spits him out ten days later. Even after several trips and in spite of all the advice, he is still paying vet bills for sick buffalo, still paying for new roofs for distant houses, still buying motorcycles for unseen relatives and still getting dumped by the love of his life once his money runs out.

That is how it was for me on my first few visits and I made just about every mistake there was to make and fell for every line. Of course, if I knew then what I know now, things would have been different. Perhaps.

The second comment was expected:
"I'm going to take this book home to show my friends, because they don't believe me when I tell them about Pattaya."
To anyone who has never been here and seen the place for themselves, Pattaya is almost impossible to describe. With truth and logic the first casualties, the reality is that here, men are no longer the predator but the quarry, no longer the hunter but the hunted. Recounting your Pattaya exploits to the uninitiated back home loses its thrill when you are continually met with looks of disbelief.

The third comment was rather surprising. It was something I wrote merely as an afterthought and I didn't think many readers would even notice. In the concluding chapter I admitted, "there is one place in Thailand that I hate more than anywhere else on the planet - the departure lounge at *Don Muang* airport." I would like one *baht* for every guy who has subsequently told me that they feel exactly the same way. Going by reader's reaction, that departure lounge must be the most depressing place in the world. One guy actually confessed he was in tears as he boarded the plane home.

The reason is simple. Pattaya is such a 'fun' town that it can be addictive - more addictive than nicotine or alcohol. Sitting in the departure lounge, the withdrawal symptoms can be acute with the visitor realizing that there is no turning back - he must get on the plane and he must go home. But 'reality' and the 'real world' will never be the same again. Suddenly, the weather back home seems exceptionally cold, wet and miserable. Suddenly, the girl in the office or the local pub, the one who he has been trying to chat up for the last six months, is not as pretty as he previously thought.

So why not simply enjoy the place and forget about trying to understand it? Because the Pattaya addiction can get you down if you let it. It can defeat you if you let it and, in the final analysis, it can break you if you let it. Knowledge is power and the more you understand how and why something works, the more chance you have of defeating it, working with it or enjoying it. Many foreign men come to Thailand, make fools of themselves, fall in love and marry after a two-week whirlwind romance. Considering the number of those marriages that end in disaster, they would have all benefited from more knowledge. Learn first, fall in love later.

I despise the term 'sex tourist' and for that reason, this is the only time I will use it in this book. In my opinion, it is a misnomer. The Thai Government and even your own government may pigeonhole you as such, you may even believe it yourself, but the truth is that no rational person would go to all the trouble and expense of travelling to Thailand purely to indulge in sex. Simple economics. Divide the total amount of money spent on the vacation by the number of sexual encounters to discover it would have been cheaper to stay home and visit a local massage parlour.

My research shows that the 'sex' is merely the bait, the sales gimmick, and men who say that is all they are here for are kidding themselves. They are more likely to be seeking the attention and affection of an attractive woman rather than the physical act itself. This is evidenced by the number of men who fall in love, the number who, after only one trip, want to sell up everything back home and move to

11

Thailand, the number who send buckets of money to a girl they hardly even know and, tragically, those who believe that life has no more meaning once they are discarded by the object of their devotion.

In his *Bangkok Post* review of *Money Number One*, Bernard Trink wrote, "Hutchison might have pointed out that much of what he suggests unique to Pattaya applies to Bangkok as well." Since then, I've learned that Mr Trink's view is indeed correct and what applies in Pattaya bars also applies to other entertainment areas throughout Thailand. Investigating them all would require more time and more money than I'm willing to spend so I am content to take the word of others. Accordingly, if you are reading this in a bar in Bangkok, Phuket, Chiang Mai or some other tourist destination, you can, relative to the general advice offered, substitute the name of your location for Pattaya.

Furthermore, although I personally know nothing about the gay scene here or anywhere else in the world, I've been assured by reliable sources that if you substitute the words 'bar boy' for 'bar girl' throughout this book, the story is virtually the same thing.

This revised and updated edition is entitled *Money **Still** Number One* because, even though the physical appearance of Pattaya has changed dramatically over the last three years, the folding stuff has not slipped from its top ranking in the hearts and minds of the population. Its domination is unchallenged - MONEY is STILL and will always be NUMBER ONE.

> *Seeking confirmation, I asked the bar girl if it was indeed true that money is number one. Her response of, "Not true. For me, fa-lung number one," sent me into deep shock until she restored my faith by smiling and adding, "because they give me money."*

Don't think that writing a book like this is easy. It involves hours upon hours of painstaking research, sitting in bars, dives and seedy rooms night after night, forcing yourself to speak with some of the most beautiful women in Thailand and some of the not so beautiful.

It means fighting a losing battle against alcoholism to the extent of writing for hours before realizing that you've been using the wrong end of the pen. It means developing theories about places and people then having to test them out to make sure the strategy works more than just the one time. Consequently, it means making mistakes, faux pas, goofs and blunders because you did not follow your own advice and instincts. It means being a stupid *fa-lung*.

Nevertheless, I don't think my love of Thailand will ever wane. On the contrary, the more I learn about the place, the more I learn about the people, the more I understand how the system works (or doesn't), the more intrigued I become. I still do not claim to be an expert because there is no such person as an 'expert' on Thailand. Here, experience is the only teacher and the class lasts a lifetime, but the learning process certainly makes life interesting. So, let's get stuck into it. Pull up a bar stool, order yourself a drink and pay attention. The Pattaya School of Hard Knocks is back in session.

CHAPTER 2

The Place

"Pattaya is like Disneyland,
except the rides are better!"

Pattaya is a city of approximately 70,000 permanent residents, 120,000 cars and 300,000 motorbikes, perfectly situated at only two hours drive from Bangkok airport depending on who is driving the vehicle. It is on the beach, compact and has everything a tourist could possibly need or want. And it is booming. New hotels, apartment blocks and businesses are springing up at a remarkable pace. The new motorway is almost finished and once the new airport south of Bangkok is completed, it will be a mere ninety minute drive away.

According to Tourism Authority of Thailand figures, in 2001 Pattaya received a total of 3.86 million visitors staying an average of 4.33 days and spending an average of 3,016 *baht* (about US$75) per person per day. This contributed a total of about 32.72 billion *baht* (US$815 million) to the Thai economy.

In spite of its popularity, the foreign press and travel writers have had a field day 'Pattaya Bashing', describing it as sleazy, dangerous and a haven for paedophiles, drug addicts and criminals. This garbage is written by journalistic hacks who spend a few days here and

14

sensationalize their copy in order to sell newspapers. The people who live here and those who visit the place often know that telling the truth would sell more plane tickets than newspapers or magazines.

Wherever you may travel in the world, there is nowhere like Pattaya. Geographically, it may be located in Thailand, but it is not Thai. Outwardly, it may have the appearance of being very European or very American, but it is not. Pattaya is a confluence of cultures, both East and West, Thai and non-Thai. It would be a mistake to judge the place by its appearance and an even greater error to judge the Thai people or rural Thailand by what you see and hear during a short holiday here.

A procession of Thai Interior Ministers, the Tourism Authority of Thailand (TAT) and the up-market Pattaya business community have been trying to improve Pattaya's international image. The place is being promoted as a family destination and a 'complete' holiday for all. Although their cause is noble, men who come here for the nightlife are accused of being 'low class' tourists and therefore unwelcome. I suspect the reason is these 'low class' tourists spend their money at the grass roots of Thai society and not in the expensive businesses owned by the already rich and powerful elite.

In any case, many families, couples and unattached foreign women do come here and have a very enjoyable time. Unlike many bar areas in other parts of the world, the bar girls of Pattaya treat foreign women incredibly well and, as for children, the Thai girls are crazy about them. The girls will play with them, keep them amused, dote over them and generally take better care of them than professional baby-sitters. The kids can have a great time.

A travel agent in Australia even promoted 'Honeymoon Package' deals to Pattaya. I have no idea how successful the promotion was, but would be interested in the divorce statistics of the happy couples who took up the offer. Bringing your wife to Pattaya is like taking a bucket of water to the Pacific Ocean.

MONEY *Still* NUMBER ONE

For the foreigner (normally written as *farang* but in Pattaya it is pronounced *fa-lung* and I make no apology for using this phonetic translation throughout this book), Pattaya can be a cheap holiday or an expensive one. If you have $s to throw around you will have the time of your life. Even with a limited budget, you can still enjoy yourself - if you know what you are doing. Through the course of this book I hope to show you how to be sensible with what resources you have.

I laugh at the guys who come here for ten days with seemingly an endless supply of cash and a pressing desire to throw it all away as quickly as possible. There is no shortage of people here eager to accept their money but when you ask them later what they thought of the free-spending foreigner, they all say the same thing: "Stupid *fa-lung!*"

When to Come

Weather-wise, between May and November it is very hot and wet. This is called the 'low season' because there are fewer tourists about and business is slow. Airfares are usually lower, accommodation is plentiful and room rates are cheaper. From December to April, called the 'high season', it is usually hot although December can be pleasantly cool, especially around Christmas. There are many more tourists about, escaping the cold in their home countries, and hotels are often heavily booked. If you plan to be here during this period, ensure that you book a room well in advance and reconfirm your booking before leaving home. Some Thai hotel managers have the annoying habit of forgetting.

TIP

Organize your holiday so that you avoid arriving in Bangkok on a Friday. The traffic is bad at the best of times, but between noon and midnight on Friday, the road to Pattaya (as well as every other road in Bangkok) is choked with cars. Similarly, your outward journey should be planned to also avoid Bangkok on either Friday or Sunday evenings.

For most single men, especially those whose passions extend no further than nocturnal activities, any time is a good time to come to Pattaya. The population of bar girls expands and contracts in proportion to the number of tourists so many men prefer to be in Pattaya during the low season when it is not so crowded. Bars and places of entertainment often heavily discount their prices to attract the fewer customers and even the bar girls are vulnerable to a bit of bargaining.

TIP

On your first trip to Pattaya it is wise to pre-book a room even if only for your first two days. You will at least be assured of a bed while you check out other places to stay for the rest of your trip. If the hotel is to your liking, it is easy to extend your booking. Changing hotels, though, is not a bad idea as you will find out in a later chapter.

Songkran

Special mention must be made of *Songkran* (Thai New Year) which, in Pattaya, is held from the 12th to the 19th of April. It is also called the 'water festival' so bring only light, casual, quick drying clothes with you. *Songkran* is one week of sheer madness. Many of Pattaya's permanent residents (the smart ones) take advantage of this time to leave and go for a week's holiday. For those people who choose to stay, it means being continually wet for seven days. Not just damp - totally soaking, dripping wet. It is fantastic fun but you must have a strong sense of humour and a strong tolerance for water.

It is also a time to take extra care on the roads. In 2001, throughout Thailand there were 554 deaths and over 34,000 injuries in vehicle accidents during the *Songkran* festival. These accidents were attributed to a combination of alcohol and the throwing of water. Around 80% of the accidents involved motorcycles so take the hint.

If you come to Pattaya for *Songkran*, do everyone a favour and bring some common sense with you. Do not throw or fire a blast of water at anyone riding a motorcycle. The water can blind them for a few seconds and anything can happen.

On a more serious note, I have made it a rule only to spray water over bar girls, those street kids who for most of the year annoy me by trying to sell me chewing gum or cigarette lighters, people in wheelchairs and people taking anti-diarrhoea medication. As you can see, my strategy is to pick on those who are least able to fight back.

The last day of the festival, the 19th, is the craziest day of all and has to be seen to be believed. Most of the local Thai population participate and begin the fun from early morning. The streets are awash with water and powder and traffic along the main thoroughfares comes to a standstill. Note that this is the only day that you are allowed to wet the local police officers. Personally, I would not take the risk of attracting the attention or angst of any policeman by dousing him with water, but the Thais seem to extract twelve months of emotion on the hapless constabulary.

In the month prior to *Songkran* 2002, an interesting article appeared in the *Bangkok Post* declaring that, "Police have been banned from using water guns to shoot at passers-by during the *Songkran* celebration." Apparently, the Police Chief was concerned they might get confused and use their real firearms by mistake. It is extremely worrying to think that Thai police do not have the capacity to differentiate between a large, pink, plastic, star-wars type water pistol and a small, heavy, metallic side-arm.

In order to curb the mayhem, the *Pattaya Mail* reported, "Pattaya police issued a strong warning to all residents and tourists celebrating the *Songkran* festival that anyone found using ice, dangerous items like home-made water guns from PVC pipes, dirty water, or powder of any kind will be fined 2,000 *baht*. The warning stated that drunk and disorderly behaviour and any form of sexual harassment will also face strong penalties and a hefty fine. Police ask that everyone respect the traditional values of *Songkran* and Thai culture." This was a waste of time, a waste of breath and a waste of ink. Politicians may grandstand about the horrific cost to the Nation of the water-throwing and powder-painting but they will not solve the problem by wishy-washy unenforceable laws about the size of the cannon or the water temperature.

The way to survive *Songkran* is to have a strong sense of humour, a strong tolerance for water and be prepared. Take extra care on the streets. Do not plan on catching *baht* taxis anywhere. It is faster to walk. Go out only when necessary and when you do go out, dress in light, casual, quick drying clothing. Expect to get a total soaking so when you are hit with water, don't get upset or angry. Don't wear a wristwatch unless it is waterproof to sixty metres. Better still, don't wear a watch. Similarly, leave the mobile phone and camera at home. Put your cash into a re-sealable watertight plastic bag and, if you are a smoker, do the same with your cigarettes and lighter. Anything else you desperately need to take with you, keep in plastic bags. I use several plastic bags as the water always seems to penetrate the outer one.

How to Get Here

Obviously, if you are sitting at a bar in Pattaya reading this, you have already solved the problem of getting here without any help. In case you are interested, you may like to know some other ways of going about it and any inherent pitfalls. Getting to Pattaya from Bangkok's Don Muang airport is easy with several alternatives.

TIP

When you leave the aircraft make sure you take your boarding pass stub with you. Thai Immigration requires you hand over your passport, arrival card AND your boarding pass at Passport Control. Don't ask me why.

Limousine

If money is no object or you have a few people to share the cost, the most convenient way to travel is by the Thai Airways Limousine service available at the airport. The trip is comfortable and the car will take you all the way to your hotel. The cost is around 2,500 *baht* which includes the motorway tolls. Check when you book.

Taxi or Private Vehicle

Taxis, with or without meters, and private operators will be only too happy to take you to Pattaya. BE CAREFUL if you travel in an unlicensed taxi or private car. Here is some advice:

1 As far as practicable, try to avoid travelling alone. Talk to other passengers on the plane or at the airport and see if anyone else is also going to Pattaya. There is bound to be someone to share the car/taxi as well as the fare. Safety in numbers.

2 Negotiate the fare before getting into a vehicle. The tout will begin by asking for something around 2,000 *baht*. At the time of writing, a reasonable fare to Pattaya by taxi is 1,500 *baht* which should include the Airport Expressway toll - 40 *baht* - and the Bangkok-Chonburi Motorway toll - 55 *baht*. That is the quickest route to Pattaya.

3   If the tout tells you to follow him to the vehicle, which will be parked somewhere in the vast parking lot, don't! Ask him to bring the car to you in the front of the airport. Never leave yourself open to be ambushed in some dark corner of the car park.

4   When the car arrives, ask the driver if it is the same vehicle that will be taking you all the way to Pattaya. It is common practice for the car waiting at the airport to be only the delivery vehicle to take you to their office where you transfer to another car which then takes you the rest of the way. No real problem, just scary the first time.

5   If you do not have much luggage, do not put it in the trunk of the car. Keep it on the seat beside you and never leave it unattended.

Bus

Air-conditioned buses go to Pattaya direct from the airport. The cost is 200 *baht* but at the time of writing there are only three per day, leaving at 9:00am, 12:00noon and 7:00pm. If this is convenient, book your ticket at the Airport Limousine Office, Counter 7 in Terminal 1.

From the Eastern Bus Terminal at Ekamai, air-conditioned buses leave for Pattaya every thirty minutes between 5:00am and 10:00pm. The current fare is 90 *baht*. The taxi fare to Ekamai from Don Muang airport is approximately 300 *baht* plus 50 *baht* airport surcharge. If you do not have a lot of luggage, take an airport taxi to Morchit Skytrain Station. This will cost around 100 *baht* plus 50 *baht* surcharge. (To avoid the surcharge, head up to the 'Departure' section and catch a taxi that has just dropped someone off.) Morchit Skytrain station is equipped with escalators up to the platform and the comfortable air-conditioned train takes about twenty minutes to travel across town to Ekamai Station for a fare of 40 *baht*. Ekamai Skytrain Station (Exit 2) is right beside the Bus Terminal. Total cost to Pattaya is about 280 *baht*.

Between 5:00am and 7:00pm buses go to Pattaya from the Northern Bus Terminal at Morchit, departing every thirty minutes. The taxi fare from the airport is again around 100 *baht* plus 50 *baht* surcharge. Morchit Bus Station is very large and there are actually two terminals within the complex. From January 2004, the bus station is undergoing renovations meaning that you buy your ticket from the booth just inside the main entrance of Morchit 1. The current fare is either 94 or 97 *baht* depending on which route the bus takes. Your quickest option is to then go through the exit directly behind you, squeeze between the first couple of rows of parked buses, jump through the hole in the fence separating terminals 1 and 2, slide through another row of parked buses and look for Gate 78 at the far right end of the platform. Good luck.

All the bus services mentioned above terminate at the bus station in Pattaya North Road. The three Airport-direct buses stop at the Limousine Service Office about 200 metres further down the road. To get to your hotel it will be necessary to catch a Pattaya taxi, commonly called a '*Baht* Bus'. Many *Baht* Buses wait at the bus station and travel a set route for 20 *baht* per person.

If your hotel is on Beach Road or Second Road, this is a good option. Simply press the buzzer when you want to get out. If you don't have a clue where your hotel is, ask one of the drivers who will take you directly for a fare starting at 40 *baht*. Negotiate. It depends how far the hotel is from the bus station, but the maximum fare for one-way group transfer from North Pattaya to anywhere else in the Greater Pattaya area is 120 *baht*. That is for a maximum of five people, NOT each!

Train
If you arrive into Don Muang airport in the early hours of the morning, do not have much luggage and are in no great rush to get to Pattaya, a very cheap alternative is to take the train. Inside the terminal building, follow the signs to the Railway Station across the elevated walkway and descend the ramp to the platform signposted 'Bangkok'. Buy a ticket to Hualampong Station at the ticket booth on the platform (regular services; fare 10 *baht*).

At Hualampong, the only train of the day to Pattaya departs at 6:55am. The fare is 31 *baht*. If you want a shower before boarding the Pattaya train, there are good facilities in Hualampong. Cost is 10 *baht*. The journey time from the airport to Hualampong is between 45 and 90 minutes depending on whether you board an express train or the 'milk run' so, if you are not on a train from the airport by 5:30am, you run the risk of being stuck at Hualampong.

The train to Pattaya takes about four and a half hours and Pattaya Railway Station is a little out of town but there is usually a *Baht* Bus hanging around the station at the time of arrival. The *Baht* Bus fare to Central Pattaya is about 50 *baht*.

Like most people, if you have just got off a long flight, the thought of travelling for another six hours to get to Pattaya is ridiculous.

Getting Back

The return trip from Pattaya back to Bangkok airport is easier still. I have found the most convenient method is to book a minibus from any hotel or travel agency. The minibus will pick you up from wherever you are staying and take you direct to the airport. The cost is 350 *baht* with the first one departing at 6:00am and the last one at 7:00pm. Make sure you book at least a day in advance.

Alternatively, two buses per day, departing at 9:00am and 1:00pm, leave from the Pattaya North Road Bus Terminal going direct to the airport. The fare is 200 *baht*.

Most Bangkok-based taxis looking for fares back to the capital will take you to the airport for 800 *baht*. There are many signs around town advertising this 24-hour service. Private operators charge 1,000 *baht*. Before booking either, confirm that the price includes all the motorway tolls.

Whatever method you choose, leave Pattaya a good five hours before your flight departure time. Most airlines now require passengers to check in two hours before their flight, leaving a safety zone of three hours to get to the airport. Don't forget to save 500 *baht* for the airport departure tax.

Places to Stay

Pattaya has many excellent hotels, apartments, and boarding houses. You can stay in one of the multi-star, big name hotels if that is your preference. Mid-range hotels are very good at 500 to 900 *baht* per night, depending on the season. Budget hotels start at around 300 *baht* per night and, although the serviced rooms may be small, are usually clean and comfortable.

TIP

Be warned that some up-market hotels will charge you extra if you bring an 'overnight guest' back to your room. It is a good idea to ask at reception before you book in. Secondly, if you are in Pattaya over the New Year period, some hotels 'require' that you pay (usually around 1,000 baht per person) to attend their New Year's Eve Party. This is whether you go or not. Again, check with reception first.

If you plan to stay for a month or more, apartments, boarding houses and pubs charging between 5,000 and 10,000 *baht* for the month are very economical.

For experienced travellers, what I'm about to say should be automatic but I will reinforce it anyway. Before booking any room, check it out. Feel the bed and switch on the fan and/or air conditioner, firstly to see if they actually work and secondly to see if they make any noise. There is nothing worse than trying to sleep with a noisy fan or air con clattering away all night. Also check that the toilet flushes and the shower supplies adequate, clean water.

Also check there is no karaoke bar or bar with a nightly live band nearby. Although the brick and cement plaster construction of most buildings is reasonably soundproof, the din from some drunk *fa-lung* screaming 'My Way' at the top of his lungs can penetrate three feet of reinforced concrete. And Thai bands know no volume setting apart from 'maximum'.

TIP

At any time of the year except perhaps around Christmas, ensure that you book a room with an air-conditioner. Thailand can get pretty hot and, for anyone not used to it, fans just do not ease the heat or humidity. Rooms with air conditioners start at around 400 baht per night.

Almost all hotels will ask for payment or partial payment in advance. If you are going to pay by credit card, they may wish to copy your card details. This is standard practice due to many hotels being caught in the past by guests leaving without checking out, saying goodbye or paying the bill.

TIP

If you are paying by credit card, either in the hotel or when shopping, do not let the card out of your sight. Credit card fraud is rife, with fake cards being produced in vast numbers. The details of the fake cards come from real cards and the most common method is for gangs to enlist the assistance of those who handle credit cards on a regular basis to make impressions of the cards.

TIP

If you are visiting Pattaya for the first time or are unfamiliar with the place, upon arrival at your hotel make sure you grab some of their business cards. Whenever you leave your room, take one of the cards with you. Why? Because you would not be the first fa-lung who has forgotten the name of his hotel when he has ended up tired and emotional in the wee small hours of the morning. Strange place + grown man + alcohol = "What the hell is the name of my hotel?"

Personal Safety

All countries have their share of dishonest people and Thailand is no exception. Some tourist guides warn that Pattaya has a reputation for being a less than safe destination for travellers. This is probably because any place that attracts around four million tourists a year is sure to also attract the criminal elements who follow the money. There is certainly a criminal element present as newspaper reports will verify. For the average mug punter though, if he doesn't go looking for trouble, he probably won't find any. I can honestly say that personally, I have never felt threatened while walking around Pattaya at any time of the day or night.

This is not to say that something untoward can not happen. Make personal safety Number One! Be sensible at all times. Pickpockets prowl many crowded places and a bag dangling from a wrist or shoulder is a tempting target for thieves who operate on foot or on motorcycles. If you do carry a bag, carry it on your side away from the road when walking alone or between the two of you when walking with a friend. This makes it more difficult for a speeding motorcyclist to snatch it from you.

His wife woke him at 3:30am to tell him that her monthly period had come on suddenly and she was out of panty-liners. Being a devoted husband, he got dressed and walked the short distance to Tops Supermarket to purchase some. Walking along Second Road on the way back to his room, a motorcycle carrying two Thai youths sped past and the passenger snatched the plastic bag from his hand. A little shaken, he walked back to Tops and bought another pack.

After telling his wife of the incident, she asked why he did not call the police. "What for?" he laughed. "It cost me 25 baht but I would pay 100 baht just to see the look on their faces once they stopped to see what goodies were in the bag."

Don't walk alone in dimly lit areas at four o'clock in the morning. If your hotel has a safety deposit facility, leave all your travel documents, valuables and extra money there, not in your room. Only carry enough money on you for your immediate needs and don't go flashing it about for the entire world to see. This is especially important if you have an 'overnight guest' in your room. Hotel staff are generally honest, but the sight of a pile of cash sitting on the dressing table may be too much temptation for a desperate employee or bar girl.

TIP

If you hide money in a 'very safe place' in your room, don't forget where you put it! One guy accused his bar girl companion of stealing several thousand baht from his room. She denied it, he ranted and raved, the police were called and the situation became very nasty. Three days later, while dressing to go out, he noticed there was something stuffed into the toe of one of his shoes. He pulled out the wad of notes he had hidden while he was drunk and subsequently accused the girl of stealing.

Thailand has its share of confidence tricksters who come in a variety of shapes, sizes and nationalities. They are always very charming and usually approach you and engage in polite conversation. Many tourists see this as an excellent opportunity to talk and mix with a friendly local. The truth is that Thai people are naturally shy and rarely go out of their way to talk to foreigners. The golden rule is, if a Thai person does approach you and appears overly eager and friendly with offers of help or advice, you can be fairly certain they are up to no good.

Be very wary of anyone (Thai or foreigner) who desperately needs to 'borrow' money from you because of some misfortune that has recently befallen him. You will not get the money back no matter how sincere he appears to be or how pathetic his tale of woe.

Tony was drinking at a bar with his Thai wife. Shortly after she went off to get something to eat another Englishman, who called Tony by name, approached him

27

and behaved as if they were lifelong friends. Tony could not recall ever meeting the guy but, when you meet people in bars, a lack of recollection can be easily explained. Anyway, he knew what hotel Tony was staying in and he bought a round of drinks. The guy went on to explain that he was in trouble as his girlfriend had left him and cleaned out his apartment and bank account. Could he borrow 1,000 baht until tomorrow? What is your room number? I'll bring it to your room before noon tomorrow. Thanks mate. He then paid his bill at the bar using the borrowed money and left. Later, Tony's lady returned and asked who was the fa-lung that he was speaking to. He said that he did not really know. Why do you ask? "Because," she answered, "he came up to me on the street and asked what your name was, what country you come from and what hotel we stay in."

The main danger in Pattaya is from cars and motorcycles. Be careful when walking around as many of the streets are devoid of footpaths. If they do exist, the footpaths are often taken up with stalls, hawkers, goods of all description or parked motorcycles and cars. This forces the pedestrian to use the roadway. Do not think, just because the road is ONE WAY, that motorcycles can not come at you from the other direction. Motorcycles go everywhere in Pattaya - on footpaths, beaches, up stairs, down escalators, through restaurants. Nothing is impossible for a motorcycle. Crossing a road is particularly dangerous. Look in every direction, not just towards the oncoming traffic, and never be in a hurry.

If you think that the danger from motorcycles is a joke, take a mental note of all the girls with scars on their arms and/or legs. When you get a chance, ask one how she got the scar. In ninety-eight percent of the cases, the scar will be the result of a motorcycle accident. One percent will be from various biting insects with the remaining one percent from self-inflicted wounds. It seems that some Thai girls are capable of becoming rather self-destructive when they suffer from depression or a broken heart.

MONEY *Still* NUMBER ONE

It was 3:00am and the four Thai girls fought over which one of them would drive the motorcycle they were all attempting to ride. The four of them were blind drunk and the argument was over which of them was the least drunk. Eventually it was decided and, with not a safety helmet in sight, the giggling quartet mounted the 125cc bike for the trip home.

In 2002, the *Bangkok Post* reported:

"A new study suggests many Thai motorcycle owners are simply accidents waiting to happen. The survey is by Chulalongkorn University, Honda Motors and the US Head Protection Research Laboratory. Here is what it says: 90% of motorcyclists in accidents have had no bike-riding training, just one in a thousand have passed any sort of recognised driving course and four of ten are drunk."

Travelling About

As soon as possible, obtain a map (available free in most hotels or tourist agencies) and familiarize yourself with the layout of the place. It is unbelievably easy to find your way around. There are many free magazines, newspapers and other publications which contain maps and provide plenty of tourist information. They are also good if you are looking for new and interesting places to go.

Baht Buses

Baht Buses, also called '*Baht* Taxis' (in Thai '*rot song taew*' which literally means 'car - two rows'), are an efficient and cheap means of getting around. Even so, *Baht* Buses figure prominently in the topic of conversation between foreigners, both tourists and expats alike. For many years now, the English language newspapers have printed letters to the editor from disgruntled foreigners complaining about being ripped off by *Baht* Bus drivers. Many complaints to the Tourist Police were about the same matter. The problem was that the fare for travel within the Pattaya area was always 5 *baht* per person. Foreigners were consistently being charged 10 or 20 *baht* and, while many of them simply accepted that there was a '*fa-lung* price' and a 'Thai price', others realized that the extra charge was a form of extortion.

The problem has finally been solved using typical Thai ingenuity. Now displayed inside each vehicle is a sign stating, 'The regular fare of mini bus in Pattaya is not over 10 *baht* per person according to the law of enforced by the department of land transport'. The solution was to simply double the fare. But (and here is the cunning bit), due to the generosity, benevolence and gooey-gooey niceness of Pattaya's *Baht* Taxi drivers, they still charge their Thai passengers only 5 *baht*.

No longer are foreigners expected to pay double fare simply because they are foreigners. They now pay the correct fare and Thais are given a 50% discount. Of course, if you happen to be travelling with a Thai companion, he or she will also be required to pay the higher fare so that the driver can be seen to be evenhanded and not because he knows that you will be paying for your companion's trip anyway.

TIP

It is still possible for fa-lung to get away with paying the 5 baht 'Thai price' on the Baht Taxis. You may wonder why bother trying to save a paltry 5 baht. Well, it is not the money, it is the principle and personally I resent being charged double simply because I am 'different'. If you want to play the game, read on.

1. *Try to avoid getting on a Baht Bus that does not already have passengers on it. Many local Thais avoid this which is a good indication that it is not a good idea. I believe that the reasoning behind it is that the driver may demand a higher fare by saying that he made a special trip for you and taken you somewhere that he had not intended to go.*

2. *Make sure that you always carry small change with you, particularly 5 baht coins. You would be surprised just how many drivers do not have change for your 20, 50 or 100 baht notes. If you hand over a 10 baht coin or note, you will definitely not receive any change.*

3. *When you reach your destination, press the buzzer as late as possible so that the taxi stops a short distance past where you actually wanted to get off. Pay for your ride by placing the exact fare into the driver's hand. Don't look at him, don't ask how much he wants, don't ask if the fare is correct, don't talk, don't discuss, don't argue, don't barter. Simply hand over the 5 baht, turn around, check for traffic and walk back to your destination. At this point, should he want to argue with you, he will have to either leave the vehicle or reverse against the flow of traffic. The drivers very rarely do this, especially if there are other passengers in the vehicle. If he does chase you for extra money, apologize politely and pay the extra 5 baht. NEVER get into an argument or altercation with the driver.*

4 *Avoid boarding the taxis that wait at supermarkets,
shopping centres and bus stations, particularly those
that park outside Royal Garden, Big C and the
Jomtien-bound ones on Second Road outside the
school at South Pattaya. Even though they will
certainly take you where you want to go, they
sometimes charge as if for a private hire. Other times
they may wait until they have a full load of passengers.
This can take a while. You are better off walking past
them and flagging down a taxi already in motion.*

Tourists throughout the world are often advised to negotiate any
fares beforehand when travelling within a foreign country. This is good
advice and is generally true. For travel on a *Baht* Bus within the confines
of Pattaya City, if you know where you are and where you want to go,
this is not really necessary. In this respect, it is a good idea to quickly
familiarize yourself with the routes the buses take. The system is not
complicated.

*Riding on a Baht Bus from South Pattaya to Naklua, I
had a 10 baht coin out to pay the fare. (This is quite some
distance so 10 baht is the correct fare.) After travelling
about 200 metres along Pattaya Second Road, the bus
stopped. A fa-lung with his Thai girlfriend approached
the driver and started to negotiate the fare to the Dusit
Hotel. The fa-lung bargained the driver down to 40 baht
for the trip and looked pleased with himself as he and his
girlfriend took their seats. I noted that the Thai girl did
not say a word to help her fa-lung companion out. She
would certainly have known where the Dusit Hotel was
and the correct fare to it. (This is not uncommon
behaviour. First and foremost, Thais look after other
Thais. You will learn more about this later in Chapter 5).
Had the fa-lung taken the time to look at a map, he would
have known that the taxi was going to go right past the
Dusit in any case and the correct fare was 5 baht per
person.*

For travel on a *Baht* Bus from Pattaya to Naklua or Jomtien, the fare is 10 *baht* for both Thai and foreigners. To hire a *Baht* Bus to take you to a destination outside the confines of the Naklua-Pattaya-Jomtien area, it *is* necessary to negotiate the fare beforehand. The driver will be only too happy to take you, even to wait and bring you back if you wish, so do a bit of haggling up front.

Motorcycle Taxis

These are easily recognizable as the drivers usually wear a coloured vest with a number and an address written on the back. They cost more than the *Baht* Buses as they offer an express door-to-door service. The minimum charge (the Thai price) appears to be 20 *baht*, but always settle on a price before you start. This is the least safe means of transport and my advice is to use it only as a last resort. I have witnessed many accidents and near-accidents involving the local motorcycle taxi service. (Note: the driver wears a helmet, you do not.)

Free Bus

On Valentines Day, 2004, a six-month trial of a free bus service began as part of the administration's efforts to ease Pattaya's traffic problems. Six air-conditioned buses were to travel a set route basically following the Beach Road-Second Road one-way circuit. A special bus lane was marked for the service and a number of bus stops were designated along the route. Buses were to run every half hour between 9:00am and 3:00pm, then again between 9:00pm and 3:00am. Between 3:00pm and 9:00pm and again between 3:00am and 9:00am, the buses were to run every twenty minutes.

As expected, after only three days of operation, an urgent meeting was called between city officials and the Pattaya *Baht* Bus Mafia. One representative from the BBM complained that since the start of the service, passenger numbers were down dramatically and after just three days, drivers were facing financial hardship. An agreement was reached to change the times and frequency of the free bus service. The operating hours were reduced to 6:00am until midnight. From 6:00am until 9:00am the buses would run every twenty minutes and from 9:00am until midnight buses would run every half hour.

Pattaya's city engineering director, *Sittiparp Muangkham*, said, "I can empathize with the *songtaew* drivers and their current predicament, but it is the *songtaew* drivers that have caused much of the traffic problems, whether it is through not adhering to the traffic laws or picking up and dropping off passengers at random, unfair pricing practices or even conforming to specified routes."

Of course, some *Baht* Bus drivers began using unsavoury tactics in an attempt to disrupt the new service. Their methods included driving along the designated bus lane in the opposite direction to block the buses, harassing bus drivers causing them to take evasive action and even harassing passengers alighting from the air-conditioned bus. Such actions created much disgust and further dislike for *Baht* Bus drivers among passengers already disgruntled with their service.

"It will benefit *Baht* Bus drivers in the long run, but only if they work within the rules, have a strict code of conduct and improve their overall image and behaviour," *Sittiparp* concluded.

As expected, city officials eventually caved in to further pressure from the BBM and reduced the trial period to three months. The bus service would run for free until the end of March after which a charge for the service would be imposed.

As reported in the *Pattaya Mail*, Banglamung district chief, *Surapol Tiensuwan*, added his comments to the issue. "The *songtaew* drivers are the criminals in this case, specifically after the numerous complaints against them in the press, by residents or Thai and foreign tourists concerning their reprehensible behaviour. There is a strong ill feeling among tourists against *songtaew* drivers. Pattaya will continue with its development in tourism. Are you part of the problem or part of the solution?"

Alas, by the time you read this, the new bus service may still exist, or it may not. It may be free, or it may not. Another good idea fell by the wayside and a great opportunity for Pattaya to attract even more tourists may have gone begging.

Vehicles for Hire

There is an abundance of cars, pick-ups and motorcycles of all description and sizes for rent in Pattaya. Shop around for the best deal, but make sure you have a <u>valid International Driver's License obtained outside of Thailand</u> and take out solid, watertight insurance. You may be asked to leave your passport with the rental agency as a security measure. Never do this! Make a photocopy if necessary, but never hand over your passport to anyone except a uniformed police officer or other legitimate Thai authorities. If the owner refuses to rent you a vehicle without your passport as security, find one who will.

My strong advice is not to drive any vehicle in Thailand but, if you insist, then heed this warning. Just because you are the world's best driver and have not had an accident in forty years, don't assume that everyone else is. Before you decide whether to drive or not, sit for five minutes and watch the traffic in the streets of Pattaya. It can be a very sobering experience. It may also lead you to believe that there are no road rules in Thailand. There are rules, it is just that no-one follows them and nobody seems to enforce them.

You may also notice that many road users appear to have no fear of death. They seem to think that they will live forever and nothing could ever happen to them. Statistics show otherwise and road accidents are proving to be an effective method of population control.

If you are driving a vehicle involved in a traffic accident, any accident, remember that you are a *fa-lung* and therefore it is likely to be your fault. Why? Because nine times out of ten, you will be the only one involved who has any money. At the least, the police could withhold your passport until you settle with the owners of any other vehicles involved. If your visa expires while they hold your passport, you have an added 'overstay' problem and can be jailed. Injured parties will expect to be paid the costs of medical treatment plus substantial compensation. The cost of repairs, medical treatment and/or legal representation *will* be astronomical. This is assuming you are not one of the 2.3 people per day who are killed in traffic accidents in Pattaya. But don't take my word for it, ask any long-term foreign residents.

Walking

Walking around pattaya is an adventure. Many cynics suggest it is impossible but it is not, as long as you are careful. It also helps to have eyes in the back of your head. Walking is great exercise and you get to see more of the finer points of the place but Pattaya has a shortfall of pedestrian-exclusive footpaths. Those walkways which do exist are uneven, potted and loaded with obstacles for the unwary.

Whatever you do, avoid standing on any of the thousands of drain covers throughout the city. The metal in some of the older ones may be corroded or the concrete may have deteriorated leaving them unsafe when weight is applied. Your 45kg Thai girlfriend may experience no problem but the cover may give way under a 100kg plus *fa-lung* frame. Jagged steel and concrete makes a mess of human flesh.

TIP

I make it a point to always walk against the flow of traffic. This allows me to anticipate potential problems and affords time to take evasive action if necessary. More importantly, it gives me the opportunity to look directly into the homicidal eyes of the mad motorcyclist just before he sends me to oblivion.

Mention should be made of the pedestrian crossings that can be found traversing several main thoroughfares. These are only here because the men marking the centre line and other lanes, once they had finished, had several gallons of paint left over. Rather than waste it, someone got the bright idea of painting zebra crossings across the road just like the pictures he had seen in foreign magazines. These lines were for no other purpose than to use up excess paint. In many Western countries, a pedestrian crossing means that the pedestrian has right-of-way and vehicles must stop to give way. Not so in Thailand. You could find yourself severely dead if you believe that any vehicle will stop for you.

Money

Yes, you will need to bring some of this with you if your holiday in Thailand is to be a success. How much you bring depends on you. How you bring it also depends on you, but here is a quick summary of the alternatives.

Cash

This is the simplest way to bring your money as all major foreign currencies can be exchanged at the banks or currency exchanges. However, it is the least safe way.

1   DON'T bring wads of cash with you unless you are confident in your ability to protect it and your hotel has a safety deposit box facility.
2   LEAVE all but the money required for your immediate needs in your hotel's safety deposit box.
3   DON'T ever leave money in your hotel room when you go out.
4   DON'T ever go walking around with half the Bank of England in your wallet.
5   DON'T advertise your wealth or go flashing it about.
6   FIND a secure place on your person to keep your wallet and/or cash. A big thick wallet hanging out of your back pocket is an easy and tempting target for a skilled thief.

TIP

If you are going to bring US currency, make sure that you do not have any US100 dollar bills in the 1990-93 series. Apparently, there are so many forgeries of these particular notes that all the banks and money changers in Pattaya no longer accept them.

TIP

Airports and hotels invariably offer the worst exchange rates. Bangkok airport and the hotels of Pattaya are no exception. Better rates are available from banks and Currency Exchangers along the street.

Traveller's Cheques

These are much safer than cash because they can be cancelled and replaced if lost or stolen. Personally, I have found them to be a little inconvenient because:

1　Not all places accept traveller's cheques.
2　When purchasing them, there is usually a fee.
3　When exchanging them, there may be a commission.
4　To spend or exchange them, you need to show your passport. I do not like carrying my passport around with me at any time.

ATM and Credit Cards

An internationally linked credit or debit ATM card is much more convenient. Thailand has many 24-hour ATM outlets that accept a variety of cards. There are some precautions that you should take and some pitfalls that you should be aware of:

1　BEFORE leaving home, check with your bank that your card will be accepted in Thailand.
2　COPY down all the details of your account (NOT your PIN number), the details on your card and the telephone number in the case of a lost or stolen card. Keep this in a safe place. Photocopying the front of your card is also a good idea.
3　DON'T rely on one card or account as your sole source of funds while you are here. Have a backup plan, spare cash or another card in case of emergency. It has been known for some of the older ATM machines to damage the magnetic strip on some credit cards. If this happens, the card is useless.
4　THINK ahead. Don't ever assume that you will just be able to stroll down to the nearest ATM and get money any time you need it. Electronic systems are prone to problems and machines here sometimes have 'communication' problems or run out of money. This is most prevalent on Sunday nights and the first and last days of each month (pay days).
5　DON'T go to the ATM and withdraw bundles of cash at three or four o'clock in the morning, especially if you are drunk or alone. That is asking for trouble.

Food

The food in Thailand is as delicious as it is varied. Almost every country that boasts food worth eating is represented by at least one restaurant. No matter what your taste, you will find it here. The fresh fruit available from street vendors is particularly delicious. If you like it hot, then the Thai food is good and relatively cheap. Anyone not used to eating spicy (hot) food should take it slowly to begin with as it could take a few days to acclimatize. Chilies are not only hot going down, but also hot coming out, if you get my meaning.

For the adventurous tourist, there is an interesting array of deep-fried bugs and insects that Thais are quite fond of. The fried grasshoppers require plenty of liquid (beer is the best) to wash them down. However, I can not bring myself to try the black beetles or other creepy-crawlies which look too much like cockroaches for my liking.

My advice is to avoid eating uncooked leafy vegetables, salads etc, and of course, do not drink the water. Bottled water is both cheap and plentiful.

There are excellent supermarkets in Pattaya including 'Big C' on Second Road opposite *Soi* 2, 'Foodland' and 'Carrefour' on Pattaya Central Road, and 'Tops Supermarket' and 'Best Supermarket' in Central Pattaya at the intersection of Second Road and Pattaya Central Road. There is a Tesco/Lotus shopping complex on Pattaya North Road as well as one situated near the intersection of *Thepprasit* Road and *Sukhumvit* Road. All have a fabulous selection of foodstuffs, wines, spirits, etc. South Pattaya has 'Friendship Supermarket' on South Pattaya Road opposite the intersection with *Soi Buakow* and a 'Big C' at the intersection with *Sukhumvit* Road.

In addition to these major retail outlets, there are innumerable other smaller supermarkets, 7-Eleven's, Family Mart's and general stores conveniently situated all around Pattaya which can be used for emergencies and the essentials – condoms, booze and cigarettes.

Drugs

Because I value my life, health and freedom, I have nothing to do with illegal drugs and therefore know very little about the drug scene. Anybody who has been in Thailand for any length of time will tell you that many of the bar girls take methamphetamines to keep them going.

In 2002, a newspaper reported that an estimated 100,000 methamphetamine pills were consumed daily in Chonburi province. The heavily publicised 2003 Government crackdown on drugs may have reduced this figure significantly but whether the stated aim of eradicating all drugs from Thailand was achieved or not is open to debate.

Consequently, like most places in this world, drugs can probably be found if you go out and look. My strong advice is not to look. If you are into that type of activity, then stay out of Thailand. I have no personal experience, but I believe that Thai jails are not the most hospitable places. With all the other enjoyable activities abounding in Pattaya, the only drug you should possibly consider is Viagra.

Viagra, by the way, is available over the counter at many pharmacies and some hotels for 500 baht per 100mg tablet. I have been reliably informed that 'copy Viagra' can also be purchased on the street for around 600 baht per pack of four. Make sure you consult a doctor before taking either.

Don't be fooled into participating in any illicit narcotic activity. At the least, you could be conned out of a few hundred *baht*. At its most serious, you could easily be set up for a 'sting' operation that works along the following lines: Once you make a drug purchase, you are apprehended by an accomplice of the seller posing as a police officer and threatened with all sorts of horrors. The seller then approaches you saying that he can 'fix' things with the police for 10,000 or 20,000 or 50,000 *baht*. You have the choice of either paying the ransom or spending a very uncomfortable time in Thailand for much longer than you planned.

STD's and AIDS

There are statistics available regarding the number of people in Thailand infected with STD's and those who have been diagnosed with HIV. The published statistics, if they only include the diagnosed cases, will be lower than the actual numbers because of many undiagnosed cases that have not been counted. I strongly urge you to use a condom each and every time you have sex. Although it still may not be 100% safe, it is certainly safer than not using one.

The girls do not want STD or HIV infections any more than you do, but many have a limited education when it comes to disease prevention. One girl told me that in order to prevent STD's, HIV and pregnancy, all she did was give herself a thorough washing immediately after any sexual activity. Her mother passed that little gem of information on to her and her ten brothers and sisters.

TIP

As a general rule, never have sex with a girl who does not **insist** *that you use a condom. If she does not insist with you, then it's a safe bet that she also did not insist with those who came before you. (Excuse the pun.)*

Some bar girls may proudly show you a health certificate testifying that they are STD-free. It is my humble opinion that these certificates are not worth the paper they are written on. I know that fraudulent ones can be purchased for 100 *baht*. Even if they are genuine, the certificate is only really good at the time she had the blood test. One hour after the test she could have unprotected sex and contract something.

Condoms can be purchased almost everywhere in Pattaya. Every supermarket, mini market, 7-Eleven and 24-hour convenience store sells condoms. There is no excuse. ALWAYS PLAY SAFE.

Medical Facilities

There are excellent hospitals, doctors, dentists, opticians and pharmacies in Pattaya. Most medical practitioners and pharmacists speak English. Let's hope that you never need to find out, but the medical treatment you would receive here is good.

My strong advice is that, if you ever fall ill with a stomach complaint (vomiting, diarrhoea, stomach pains etc), consult a doctor immediately. It may turn out to be a simple case of food poisoning, but the symptoms could also be an indication of something more serious. The same goes if you are bitten by an animal - any animal - see a doctor immediately. I don't care what the brochures say, rabies still exists in South East Asia.

TIP
If you need some types of dental work or require new prescription glasses, check the prices in Pattaya. Many tourists find the rates here are much cheaper than for the same service in their own countries.

CHAPTER 3

The People

"Give a man a fish and he will eat for one day.
Teach him how to fish and he will sit in a boat
and drink beer all day."

Thais are a gentle, wonderful and yet complex people. It is often difficult for foreigners to rationalize their sometimes-idiosyncratic behaviour. For every strange, oddball, confusing, illogical event that happens in Thailand, expats have a simple explanation - "This is Thailand!"

But Pattaya is not typical of Thailand. Books on Thai culture may be accurate when referring to the people in the provinces but the Thais who work in the major tourist destinations can prove the exceptions to many rules.

> *The foreigner decided to move to Pattaya but, being*
> *cautious, asked his expat friend, "Living in Pattaya, what*
> *are the pros and cons?"*
> *His friend casually replied, "A somewhat broad but*
> *accurate description of the population."*

Consequently, before you interact with the local inhabitants, there are some lessons to be learned.

Lesson One – Nationalism

Thailand is the only country in South East Asia that has never been colonized. In the past, they have even ceded territory in exchange for maintaining independence. Luckily, at the height of colonial power in Asia, the English in India, Burma and Malaya and the French in Indo-China and Cambodia found it convenient to leave Thailand as a buffer zone between them. At the outbreak of World War II, Thailand was the only Asian country to ally with Japan. As a result, the Japanese returned to Thailand the territory previously ceded to England and France.

Since the war, generally speaking, the Thais managed to keep the rest of the world at arm's length. In spite of years of internal political upheaval and turmoil (there were seventeen coups in sixty years) and in spite of economic disasters, the Thai people have slowly modernized their country - their way. Thais don't appreciate foreigners sticking their noses into what they perceive as strictly Thai affairs.

"What does this have to do with me having a great time in Thailand?" I hear you ask. Firstly, you will have a much easier time here if you always remember, when dealing with Thai people, they are extremely proud and nationalistic. They love Thailand and despite their outward friendliness and 'Thai smile', generally do not care much for foreigners. They are not xenophobic. They do not have a fear of foreigners, they simply could not care less. Nothing personal. They only like things that are Thai - Thai food, Thai music, Thai culture, Thai traditions and Thai thinking. A quick way to get a Thai off side is to continually criticize their country or way of life. A "back home we do this" or "back home it's like that" type of guy makes no friends here.

Secondly, don't meddle in Thai business. If your Thai girlfriend is involved in a heated argument or even a fight with another Thai, stay the hell out of it. Never forget, that delicate little flower beside you, the one who has managed to capture your heart, no matter what she does or where she lives, no matter how she dresses or how she speaks, is now and will always be, 100% THAI.

Lesson Two - Smiling

There has been much already written about the ever-present 'Thai smile'. Without repeating what you may already know, the important thing to realize is that a Thai, smiling, may not necessarily indicate the same thing it does when you or I smile. Westerners smile to convey happiness, amusement or a pleasant greeting. A Thai smile can mean these things plus it can also mean 'please', 'thank you', 'goodbye', 'excuse me', 'I'm sorry', or 'yes'. It can also be a way of showing embarrassment or easing the tension if a situation looks to be getting too heated.

> *My first Thai girlfriend (you will read a lot about her in these pages. She cost me a fortune but taught me many valuable lessons) and I had a heated argument one day. The argument was basically one-sided as I ranted and raved. With my blood pressure just about to blast me into lunar orbit, I looked at her – and she was smiling. This enraged me even more and I shouted at her, "Do you think that this is funny?" To cut a long story short, I calmed down, she made an insincere apology and we made up. Much later, I came to realize that she had been smiling, not because my tirade was amusing her, but because she was trying to ease the tension. Jai yen! At least, I **hope** that's why she was smiling.*

Because their smile has so many meanings, it appears that they are always smiling. In fact, two Thais silently sitting together trading smiles with each other could actually be having an in-depth conversation.

Lesson Three - Lying

One of the five Basic Precepts of Buddhism is "Do not tell untruths". In spite of this, you must always remember that Pattaya is Fantasyland and should not be taken too seriously. As well as telling lies for the all the usual reasons, Thais (and this is true of Asians in general) will sometimes lie to avoid an unpleasant situation or to avoid 'losing face'. They also want to keep you happy and if this involves telling a lie, then so be it. When you later discover that they have been less than forthright, they are usually not around to argue with.

There was once an enterprising but misguided fellow who brought a lie detector machine with him to Pattaya. Unfortunately it blew every fuse and blacked out half of the city less than five minutes into his first interrogation. He would have been better off bringing a truth detector. It would have required a lot less electricity since it would only light up when someone actually told the truth.

Sometimes, they will not actually lie in the strict Biblical sense of the word. They will simply not tell the full truth. If a bar girl answers your question with a noncommittal response of "maybe", "sometimes" or "perhaps", it usually means that the correct answer is one that you do not want to hear. In a conversation she may tell you only the things that you want to hear and conveniently leave out anything she thinks you will not like, no matter how important the information could be to you. This strategy seems to work quite well. When they do happen to tell an outright blatant lie, there is no limit to their imagination.

Once upon a time there was a guy who worked as a cook. One day his employer decided to entertain guests and ordered a roast chicken to be prepared for the meal. The cook himself was very hungry but was forbidden to eat. Eventually the smell of the roasting chicken got the better of him and, unable to contain his hunger any longer, he ate one of the legs. When he served up the chicken, minus one leg, the boss was furious and demanded to know what happened to the missing appendage. The cook replied that the chicken only had one leg to begin with. This obvious bullshit made his boss even angrier and he started beating the cook to force a confession. Even after a savage battering (excuse the pun), the cook still stuck to his 'one-legged chicken' story.

In Pattaya you will hear many 'one-legged chicken' stories.

The deceit and deception is not all one-sided by any means. I know that you, dear reader, would never think of tinkering with the affections of your wonderful companion by considering being other than 100% honest with her, but there are some *fa-lung* who do not possess your high moral standards.

Lesson Four – Reasoning and Logic

There are two theories for arguing with a Thai. Neither of them work. All jokes aside, Thais merely have a non-European way of thinking about things and use different reasoning when addressing a problem. The logic is there, but it differs from the way Westerners are taught to think.

> *I told my girlfriend that I would call her on a certain night. Something came up and I was unable to call as arranged but did call her the next evening. She was incredibly angry, saying that she waited up until 2:00am for my call. I apologized and explained that, under the circumstances, it was unavoidable. She went on to say that during the day she went out to play (illegal) cards and proceeded to lose 5,000 baht. She only played because she was angry with me. It was therefore my fault that she lost the money. Now, if that logic makes sense to any foreigner out there, please write to me and explain. (Also enclose a certified copy of your most recent psychological evaluation.)*

Thai people are also very intelligent and ingenious. Just because she has had limited formal education, don't ever think that she is not smart. Given a little time, a bar girl can worm her way into or weasel her way out of most situations. It is not something that she needed to learn. It has been bred into her over the centuries.

> *A fa-lung arrived back at his apartment to find the bedroom door blocked by a wardrobe. He forced his way in to*

discover his girlfriend in a semi-clothed state with a Thai man who was equally poorly attired. Angrily, he threw the guy out, using as much physical persuasion as he could muster. Later, his girlfriend explained that the Thai man was actually her brother who had paid her a surprise visit. On noticing that there was a foul odour coming from somewhere in the bedroom, they began moving furniture around in order to find the source. It was then that the apartment's power failed and, with no air conditioning, the pair decided to remove excess clothing in order to keep cool as they worked.

Ah, Mr Ripley, where are you when we need you? The number of concerned Thai brothers visiting their sisters in Pattaya is only exceeded by the number of monoped fowls hopping along Beach Road.

TIP
Never give your girl time to think about any proposition you may make to her. Given twenty-four hours to mull it over, she will consult with her sorority of friends – the brain trust – who will put their collective heads together and like Baldrick, come up with 'a cunning plan'. I guarantee that the result will cost you money. As a general rule, the less time she has to think over your proposition, the more chance that her response will be in your favour.

Lesson Five - Promises

Thai bar girls have excellent selective memories. I say 'selective' because anything they perceive to be to their benefit they remember, anything else, they conveniently forget.

Be very careful what you say or what you promise, because they will not forget it. You could find yourself having to make good something that you had merely mentioned in jest or said when you were blind drunk.

"The number of concerned Thai brothers visiting their sisters in Pattaya is only exceeded by the number of monoped fowls hopping along Beach Road."

My girlfriend wanted me to buy her a gold chain. I kept putting her off and avoided walking past any gold shops when I was with her. Eventually, just to shut her up, I said I would buy it next time I came back to Pattaya. I was away for two months and forgot all about it. The very day I arrived back, she frogmarched me straight to a gold shop where she had obviously been eyeing off a nice necklace. I was then reminded of my 'promise' and shamed into coughing up the $s.

Of course, any promise made to you by a Thai girl is a different matter. If they fail to deliver on that promise, they will either deny all knowledge of it or come up with the most elaborate excuse as to why they could not fulfil their obligation. All with a smile on their face.

Lesson Six – Sentimentality

The practicalities of daily survival mean that Thais are not very sentimental. They can't afford to be. If they can't spend it, sell it, eat it, wear it, live in it or ride it, they don't want it. That 100-year-old copper brooch that your great grandmother gave you on her deathbed is totally lost on a Thai. Why? Because the world copper price is very low. If it were gold, however, it would be a different story. In times of need it could be sold for the weight of the gold. Forget about its historical or sentimental value.

Similarly, that beautifully framed photo of the two of you together will last only as long as you do. After that, the photo will be removed, your image will be cut out and you and whatever good times you had together, will be forgotten. Souvenirs, keepsakes and mementos are equally as meaningless unless, of course, they are made of gold.

Any photos of previous girlfriends you may be keeping for purely sentimental reasons should be hidden away from your current flame. She will not understand your desire to keep them now that you have her.

Lesson Seven – Borrowing

It appears that, in Thailand, the word 'borrow' has exactly the same meaning as the word 'give'. Any time a Thai girl asks to 'borrow' something from you, don't expect it to be returned. Asking for it back is simply too rude to contemplate, besides being a total waste of time and effort.

When I was young and stupid I loaned a Thai girl 3,000 baht to get her out of trouble, with her promise to return it by the end of the month. Two months later, I asked her for the money. She became all flustered and walked away. My girlfriend, her friend, subsequently derided me for asking for the money because she said her friend was 'shy'.

Lesson Eight – Here and Now

Generally speaking, Thai people tend to live from moment to moment, one day at a time. They don't think too far into the future and short-term gain is seen to be far better than future promises. To put it another way, 'a bird in the hand is worth two in the bush'. For you, a foreigner, this means that they will not put too much faith in what you say you will do or what you say you will deliver sometime down the track. What is more important to them is what you are doing and delivering now.

Lesson Nine - Eating

It won't take you very long to notice that Thai people seem to have a preoccupation with eating. When they feel hungry, eating is the most important thing on their mind. While *fa-lung* usually eat three relatively substantial meals a day, a Thai will eat smaller meals up to eight times a day. They will eat any time they feel hungry (which is often). This is actually a very healthy way of life. Compare for yourself the number of fat *fa-lung* you see in Pattaya opposed to the number of overweight Thais.

Lesson Ten - Sleeping

I read somewhere that you know you have been in Thailand too long when you can sleep standing up on a bus. This is true, because I have seen it. Thais can do with little or no sleep for long periods but, when the need or opportunity arises, they can sleep anywhere – in a thumping disco, on the side of a busy road, on the back of a motorcycle or standing up in a bus.

The bar girls are very fond of sleeping and can sleep sixteen hours a day if you (and their stomachs) let them. Many foreign men complain about it but, when you stop and think, is it such a bad thing? While your girlfriend is sleeping, she is not spending (your) money. Let sleeping Thais lie.

A guy bemoaned the fact that his girlfriend was either watching TV, eating or sleeping. I replied that at least they were three inexpensive habits. If she was either shopping, bingeing or whining he would have more cause for concern.

Lesson Eleven - Drinking

Another of the five Basic Precepts of Buddhism is "Refrain from intoxicants". Many Thai males drink alcohol although you may find that many bar girls do not. Those who do can hold their own against the best and will only stop when one of the following occurs:

(a)   They run out of alcohol.
(b)   They run out of money to buy more alcohol.
(c)   They collapse into unconsciousness.

I have never personally witnessed (c). Thai parties last all night with bottles of Chivas or cheap Thai rotgut disappearing faster than last week's pay packet. Unfortunately, like the rest of the human race, some Thais can become aggressive when drunk so just be careful if you go out drinking with your extended Thai family.

Lesson Twelve – Face

Money may be the root of all evil but in Thailand, 'face' is the root of most of the negative behaviour displayed by the people. To 'lose face' means a loss of respect, being shamed or looked down on by others while 'gaining face' means gaining prestige or status in the eyes of others. Do not underestimate the importance Thais place on this. On many occasions it is the reason behind the lies or aggression.

I have heard them tell the most outrageous lies to their friends about their supposed wealth or social status. Bar girls constantly play the 'my *fa-lung* is better than your *fa-lung*' game whereby they exaggerate the amount of money their *fa-lung* earns and gives them.

His wife got her driver's license. Seeing that it was only three days between the time she applied and when the card was in her hands, he correctly assumed that she had not undergone any form of driver training or completed any recognized competency test. He bought her a cheap second-hand car as her introduction to mobile happiness.

After receiving her less than handsome gift, she was heard to say loudly in front of his friends, "My best friend have husband Denmark. She get license and after two days he buy her new car. My other best friend have husband Sweden. She have license one week then he buy her new car. I have husband Australia. Have license two week and he buy me cheap Charlie old car. No good."

That lady had lost face in front of her two best friends and nothing short of the latest in road fashion would get it back. The worst and possibly the most dangerous thing you can do to a Thai is be the cause of them losing face.

> *"Oh Lord, won't you buy me a Mercedes Benz;*
> *My friends all drive Porches, I must make amends."*
>
> Janis Joplin

Lesson Thirteen - Taboos

If you have read any book on Thailand, there will have been some mention of the taboo regarding pointing with your feet. It has been my experience in Pattaya that this has been grossly exaggerated. I have had more Thai feet and toes pointed at me than I have had hot dinners. In Pattaya, European influence is such that they do not seem to worry about 'the feet thing' too much. Do not point with your feet or pick something up with your toes but, apart from that, there is no need to be constantly on your guard for fear of offending someone. Don't worry about it. *Mai bpen rai!*

The head is regarded as sacred in Thai culture. Touching someone on the head is a big no-no. Many foreigners have the endearing habit of patting or stroking the head of their newly found love. She will usually pass it off and not show any degree of discomfort at this behaviour but, under the surface, your action will be less than appreciated. Avoid touching a Thai on the head.

Something else I found quite amusing. It appears that Thais do not like the colour black because of its association with death. Hah! There are more people wandering around Pattaya wearing black outfits than at a Sicilian funeral. Black t-shirts, black jeans, black skirts, black dresses. Check it out.

Lesson Fourteen – Asking Directions

The problem that foreigners have in getting accurate directions from locals is not unique to Thailand. It is true of all Asia. The Asian culture is such that, answering a question by saying, "I don't know", when they could reasonably be expected to know the answer, means a loss of face. It means that the other person may think they are less than intelligent. To avoid this, they will give an answer, any answer, even if it is just a guess and totally inaccurate.

I drove two charming Thai ladies up country to a place they supposedly knew very well. After several "Turn left"s,

55

"No, turn here"s and "This way better"s, I consulted my map and found that we had travelled about 100 kilometres out of our way. When I quietly but firmly pointed out their navigational error, they thought it was a great joke.

Study a map before you travel anywhere outside Pattaya. Do not rely on asking a local for directions to your place of interest. If you ask four Thais the same question, they will each point in a different direction.

The guy was driving his girlfriend and her friend up country when he became lost. Wanting to save time, when he saw a policeman standing beside the road, he pulled over and told the very reluctant girls to get out and ask for directions. They finally did so and he guessed that they were chatting away with the policeman for at least fifteen minutes before returning to the car. They both nodded enthusiastically when he asked them if they now knew where to go.
"Which way then?"
In unison, one girl pointed to the left and the other to the right.

Lesson Fifteen – Taking Photos

Be careful if you wish to take photos in and around the bar areas. Taking photos inside Go Go Bars and Short Time Bars is usually prohibited so don't even take your camera inside one of those places. The Beer Bars are generally OK about taking photos, but it is advisable to ask permission before happily snapping away. Always ask permission before taking photos of individual girls or foreigners, for that matter. Most Thai girls love having their photo taken and will be only too pleased to pose for you. You may, however, find the occasional one who, for whatever personal reason, does not appreciate it.

My friend had only been in Pattaya for a couple of days and I forgot to warn him about this. He innocently snapped a photo of an artificially-attractive silicon-enhanced Thai woman who took immediate objection to it. She stormed off and reported the incident to her mentally-challenged Neanderthal fa-lung boyfriend. He then made his way towards me and told me, in no uncertain terms, what he would do to my friend and his camera if he took another photo of his girlfriend. With knuckles dragging along the ground, he then slithered back to his cave.

Lesson Sixteen – Aggression

Any time you mix alcohol with people from very different cultures and backgrounds, there is bound to be some aggressive or violent behaviour. For a city its size, there is surprisingly very little visible violence here. Hopefully, the reason is that everybody is too busy having a good time to bother fighting each other. Whatever the reason, it is good news.

To keep it that way, avoid violence at all costs. If you do happen to witness an altercation, stay out of it. This is particularly true if the fight or argument involves Thai people. Thais are usually very placid and gentle people, however they can snap in a second and their anger knows no bounds. Thais can get deadly serious. Even if your girlfriend is involved in a foray with other Thais, stay out of it. Don't try and be John Wayne or try and act as peacemaker. You can not win. Let the Thais sort it out and then be there with a band-aid, aspirin and comforting shoulder should your ladylove require it.

To limit even the possibility of confrontation, the less you have to do with Thai men in Pattaya, the better. Alcohol can bring out the worst in people. Under no circumstances should you accept gifts of food or drink from them. Politely refuse any unsolicited offers of advice, suggestions or help. Never, ever go out on a drinking spree with, pursue an argument with or attempt to 'get tough' with a Thai man. Many a *fa-lung* has thought he has won an altercation and settled it, only to find that the Thai returns later with a few of his friends to even the score. Any time you encounter a problem, walk away or seek out the Tourist Police and let them sort it out.

57

Lesson Seventeen – Language

Many tourist guidebooks state that Thai people appreciate a foreigner who tries to speak their language. They know the language is difficult for foreigners and therefore your efforts will make a positive impression on them. This may be true in other parts of Thailand, however bar girls do not appear to appreciate foreigners who can speak and understand Thai. Yes, they know that their language is difficult and THAT IS THE WAY THEY LIKE IT! They know they can talk among themselves and you will not have a clue what they are saying.

Bar girls treat foreign men who can speak Thai differently to the 'mug' tourists. If a foreigner has learned the language, it can only mean one of two things:

(a)   He lives or works here; or

(b)   He visits so often that he has picked up the language.

In the first case, he will most probably have a Thai wife or at least a long-term Thai girlfriend. In the second case, he may not have a Thai wife, but he will have one or two girlfriends around the place. In both circumstances, it usually means that the guy is familiar with the place and therefore, "knows too much". (That is an exact quote from one bar girl.) It may also mean that he has come to the bars simply to 'chill out' or maybe to 'butterfly' a little. The chances of a bar girl extracting a large sum of money from him are not as good as if he were say, a run-of-the-mill tourist.

My friend disagrees with me on this point. One girl told him that all the girls in her bar liked him because he could speak Thai. I countered by saying that he speaks Thai very badly (similar to Jed Clampett reading Hamlet), so I think the girls were more amused than impressed.

Even though they may no longer treat him as if he were a source of revenue and seem to drop most of the feminine charms reserved for the punters, this is not to say that they will not go with a foreigner who can speak Thai. On the contrary. It is probably a relief for them because they know that they can at least have a conversation, they don't have to be on their 'best' behaviour, they don't have to lie and they are still going to be paid for their time.

If you do learn to speak Thai it is much more fun if you don't let on. Some of the girl's conversation is interesting when they think that you can not understand. Mostly though, their conversation is very mundane. It is usually about food. They can talk for hours about what they had to eat, what they are going to eat or what they would like to eat. Boring stuff.

One of my favourite tricks is to go to a bar I have never been to before and pretend that it is my first trip to Thailand, I just arrived and I'm staying for ten days. On one occasion, a girl with dollar signs in her eyes swooped on the bait. She could not speak a word of English and continually asked the mamasan what to do, how could she get me to buy her a drink and how much she should ask for should I succumb. I played totally dumb until, just before leaving, I answered all her questions in my best Thai. It is not safe for me to return to that bar.

I strongly recommend that you learn at least the basics of the language if you plan to spend a lot of time in Thailand. I will not go into the intricacies of it here as there are many books on the subject. There are a number of regional variations on the Thai language and Lao is widely spoken but it is the tonal nature of the language that makes it extremely difficult for foreigners to learn. As an example, ask a Thai to read the following sentence and then try to repeat what you heard.

ไม้ใหม่ไม่ไหมมั้ย

In English it means, "New wood doesn't burn, does it?"

CHAPTER 4

The Bars

"Just another shitty day in Paradise."

Various experts, expats and exiles suggest that there are between 500 and 3,000 bars of all descriptions in Pattaya. It is highly likely that the '500 group' missed quite a few streets, while the latter group probably started seeing double after a few hours of research. One thing is for certain - the number has doubled over the past four years.

Basically, there are three types of bars in Pattaya - Go Go Bars, Indoor Recreational Lounges (aka 'Short Time Bars') and Beer Bars. I am deliberately not going to mention any particular bar by name nor make any recommendations. This is for three reasons. Firstly, the appeal of a bar depends on your own particular tastes. What I find appealing about one establishment may turn someone else off and vice versa. Secondly, bars open, close and change hands on a regular basis. Here today - gone tomorrow. Thirdly, the quality of a bar is highly dependent upon the staff working there. Bar girls are notorious for their flightiness and the high turnover of staff is always a problem for bar owners. You may enjoy drinking at a particular bar because of the girls working there, only to return a month later to find the friendly, gorgeous little angels who stole your heart have scattered. They have been replaced by a bunch of nose-picking Noras that you would not give ten *baht* for, let alone pay a bar fine.

A 'tab' system operates at all bars. Each time you buy a drink, a docket is placed in a plastic or wooden cup in front of you. This is called your '*bin*'. When you decide to leave the bar, you merely have to say '*check bin*'. The dockets will be added up by the cashier and stapled together. The total will be written on the back and shown to you for payment.

TIP
Whenever you 'check bin' at a bar, always count up the bill yourself. I am not saying that the bars will try and cheat you, but it is much better to be safe than sorry. It has happened to me on several occasions that the actual bill was 100 baht lower than the one quoted to me. I put this down to the girls' lack of higher education in mathematics. It is surprising though, that all mistakes are in the bar's favour. Even if you are so drunk that you don't know which way is 'up', at least be seen to be adding up the bill. You should have no problem thereafter.

Some bars in other parts of the world, for example Manila in the Philippines, require that the customer sign each docket before it is placed in his bin. That way, he knows exactly how much he is being charged each time. Good idea, but it is not the case in Pattaya.

A bar-owner friend of mine attempted to start the practice at his bar. His mamasan immediately shot down the idea by explaining that it meant that each girl would have to carry a pen around with her. Too difficult. He agreed once he realized just how many pens he would lose each night.

Another friend told me that, some time ago, a bar in Pattaya did actually try this system. He had a long session one night and, since he was well known at this particular bar, put off paying his bill until the following day. (Not recommended practice.) The next day he was astounded to find that his bill came to over 2,000 baht. He complained and, going through each docket with the Thai bar manager, pointed out that some dockets carried a signature that was definitely not his own. "Yes," said the bar manager, "but you were very mao [drunk] last night so I sign for you."

You may also notice that every bar has a bell hanging in a prominent position. This is NOT to call for service, even though if you did ring it, you would get the best and fastest service you have ever seen. It should only be rung if you are feeling very generous and your wallet is weighing you down. 'Ringing the bell' means that you have just shouted a drink for everyone in the bar, including all the staff. The girls will go crazy, your popularity will soar and your finances will shrink. Don't even think about ringing the bell in jest because it will not be taken as a joke.

Most, but not all, of the ladies working behind the bar will be allowed to leave with you upon your payment of her 'bar fine'. The amount varies depending on the type of bar and the season. Usually, a '*bin*' will be written out and you will pay it when you '*check bin*' and leave the bar. Unlike parts of the Philippines and Cambodia, this bar fine does not include the girl's personal fee. That should be negotiated directly with the girl and NEVER paid in advance.

TIP
If you and one or two friends bar fine girls from the same bar, agree beforehand how much you will give each girl. The girls will certainly compare notes later so, if one received 500 baht, one 1,000 baht and one 1,500 baht, it makes the guy who paid the least look bad and the one who paid the most look stupid. The girl who received the least will have lost face and a repeat performance will cost you dearly.

Go Go Bars

These are the bars behind closed doors or heavy curtains, variously described in the press as 'Ogling Dens' or 'Chrome-pole Palaces'. They go by some very quaint, imaginative and provocative names. Many don't open until after 7:00pm, although some open as early as 2:00pm. In Pattaya, most Go Go Bars can be found in and around Walking Street, South Pattaya, but there are isolated ones all over the place. Some proudly advertise 'No Cover Charge' but I have not seen one yet that actually has a cover charge. Unescorted ladies and hawkers are not welcome in Go Go Bars.

Inside the dimly lit decor, the girls dress scantily and 'dance' around a pole or poles on a prominent lit stage. They usually wear a number attached somewhere to their limited clothing. If no clothing, it may be on one of their shoes. If a girl takes your fancy and you would like her to sit with you, it is simply a matter of quoting her number to a drink attendant. Most of the time though, all you have to do is smile at her. The girls are not as shy as their sisters in the Beer Bars outside and some can be very forthright as to what they would like to do with you, so be prepared. Some can also be very demanding when it comes to wanting you to buy them a drink and 'lady drinks' can be expensive.

Some Go Go Bars provide stage shows, usually later in the evening. One or more ladies will perform 'acts' which I won't describe here, but be assured they require a degree of sexual agility. Some Go Go Bars used to have 'short-time' rooms available but since this practice is illegal, the rooms no longer exist. (And if you believe that ...)

The bar fine for 'short time' will start at 300 *baht*. For an overnighter, the bar fines are usually 500 *baht* but may be 600 *baht* if she happens to be one of the acts on stage but can go up to 1,000 *baht*. It is a good idea to ask beforehand. The girl's professional services start from 500 *baht* for 'short time' and from 1,000 *baht* for overnight.

Having said that, most Go Go Bars drastically increase their prices during high season. This is for two reasons: Firstly, cashed-up

63

holidaymakers have no brains and secondly, it is to discourage punters from running off with the bar's star attractions. Let's face it, an empty stage is going to entice no-one to sit down. Some girls suddenly become superstars as well by demanding 2,000 to 3,000 *baht* for their services. Why? Because some men are stupid enough to pay it.

Short Time Bars

These bars are also enclosed behind doors or curtains. There may be no dancing or stage show but the girls are definitely not shy. Some of the girls are very, very, very friendly. All of the girls are very, very, very obliging. The main attraction of these bars used to be that they were discreet and provided rooms for patrons to go 'short time'. Whenever the mood took you, it was simply a matter of retiring to one of the rooms with the apple of your eye in tow to enjoy a refreshing shower, engage in some horizontal activity, have another shower then return to the bar feeling rejuvenated. It costs around 300 *baht* for the room and the girl's fee will be upwards of 500 *baht*. Best to negotiate with the girl beforehand.

Nowadays, bars providing rooms for patrons to go 'short time' are illegal so I now prefer to call them 'Indoor Entertainment Lounges'. Whatever name you use, like Go Go Bars, hawkers and unescorted ladies are not welcome inside. These bars are designed for the *fa-lung* who, for one reason or another, should not be seen in a bar. Many men who already have a Thai girlfriend (or two) visit these places when they feel the need to 'butterfly' a little.

Beer Bars

By far, the majority of bars in Pattaya are the open-air, kiosk-type Beer Bars. Since I began writing the original *Money Number One* in 1998, the number of Beer Bars in Pattaya has got to have doubled. Everywhere you look, new ones are springing up with no shortage of optimistic entrepreneurs eager to take up the challenge of running a bar. (More on that later.)

65

Beer Bars generally never close as there is always at least one member of staff in attendance. They do, however, cease serious activity once the last customer has left in the wee small hours. A currently enforced ordinance requires bars to close by 2:00am and moves were afoot to reduce this to midnight. But relax, it is a good bet that at any time of the day or night you can buy a drink at one of these bars. The real action takes place between 8:00pm and 2:00am when there will be anywhere between five and thirty beautiful girls to serve you drinks and keep you entertained.

Some of the Beer Bars have live bands performing at night and some provide karaoke for those people who consider themselves to be Elvis Presley. (Note: If you can not sing, do us all a favour. Don't!) Some have pool tables, dartboards or big-screen TVs to keep customers entertained. Even if you are alone and feel like a game of eight-ball, one of the bar girls will be happy to play. After a game or two it would be polite, but not compulsory, to buy her a drink for her time. If you like to play for money, do so at your own risk. It is surprising how a girl's game can dramatically improve once there is *baht* at stake.

Every Beer Bar has a 30,000 watt stereo system and there seems to be a competition to see which one can play the loudest music. Thais appear to believe that loud noises attract foreigners.

TIP
If you do not like the Eagles song 'Hotel California', then take earplugs with you. I have not spent a night in Pattaya without hearing this song played. As I have said before, Thais only really enjoy Thai music, but play fa-lung songs just to attract the tourists. They do seem to like 'Hotel California' though. Every bar has a copy and they play it to death.

Beer Bars are mostly found clustered together under one large roof. There are nests of them everywhere. There will be one communal toilet somewhere in the near vicinity. The use of these toilet facilities is usually not free and you may be asked to pay between three and five *baht*. The money is supposedly used for the upkeep and maintenance of the toilets but, at some places, you may question where the money really went.

> *You may notice some of the bar girls have one baht coins wedged inside their ears. This is not some weird Thai fashion, but a convenient way to carry the 'toilet money' when they get caught short.*

One disadvantage of drinking at a Beer Bar is that you can be harassed by hawkers selling everything from flowers, watches, cameras, clothing, a shoeshine to chewing gum and cigarettes. This is especially true if the bar is close to the street. Many of the hawkers are children and can be really annoying. Unless you desperately need something that they are selling, it is best to politely refuse their offers. If a watch, camera or shirt does take your fancy and you wish to do a bit of bargaining, the general rule is that the correct price is about one-third of their initial offer. If you get them down to around half the original asking price, you are doing OK.

The problem is exacerbated when a foreigner does actually buy something from one of the vendors. World satellite communication systems have got nothing on the Thai sales-network.

> *One evening, a fa-lung with a 'good heart' bought a few bunches of flowers for some of his female admirers. I did not know the guy otherwise I would have told him to save his money (Refer Chapter 6, Item 5). Within milliseconds, word had spread to every flower vendor within running distance. The bar resembled the opening Covent Garden scene from My Fair Lady. Eventually the mamasan came to his rescue and dispersed the zealous throng.*

The lottery ticket sellers can also be a nuisance. The National Lottery is held (usually) on the 1st and 16th of each month and for the week or so before the draw, the streets are full of vendors carrying wooden cases loaded with lottery tickets. The cost of a ticket is 45 *baht*. The actual price on the ticket is 40 *baht*, the extra 5 *baht* being the vendor's commission. The draw is held live on TV and if you are a total masochist, watch it. The lowest prize dividend is 1,000 *baht*, but you will only receive 970 *baht* when you go to collect. There is a 3% (30 *baht*) commission.

Bar Games

There are four main games that the bar girls enjoy playing. These are used to relieve boredom (both yours and theirs) due to communication problems. They are also used to keep you amused and keep you drinking at the bar. The girls play these games amongst themselves during slack times when there are no *fa-lung* about.

The most common game is played with dice. It comprises a wooden box with the numbers 1 to 9 painted on wooden flippers and two dice. You throw the dice and, depending on what you throw, flip over one of the wooden numbers. E.g. If you throw a 1 and a 4, then you can take either a 1, 4, or 5. If the numbers you throw have already been taken, the game is over. The idea is to clear all the numbers. Sometimes it can take a long time before someone wins. Although it is purely a game of chance, girls who have been in Pattaya a long time are experts at this game.

TIP

You do not have to be a mathematical genius to work out the probabilities of throwing a particular number. The idea is to work from the outside in. Leave the 5 and the 6 until last. The chances of throwing a particular number increase in the following order: 9-8-7-1-2-3-4-5-6.

Anyway, the true purpose of playing the game is not to win, just to fill in time between slurps of cold beer and to get acquainted with the charming hostess. NOTE: Gambling is strictly illegal in Thailand.

The second game is 'Bingo Line-up' or 'Connect 4', a game consisting of a vertical plastic frame down which you drop coloured tokens. The idea is to get 4 of your tokens together in a row (vertically, horizontally or diagonally). Unlike the dice game, this is a game of skill. Bar girls who play this game for hours each and every day become very good at playing it and they like to win. I can offer no hints as to how to win at this game. Again, gambling is strictly illegal in Thailand.

The next game is 'Jenga'. It consists of a tower of wooden blocks arranged in a hatch formation. The idea is, using only one hand, to take a block from somewhere within the stack and place it on top, thus building the tower higher. If the tower falls during your turn, you lose. This is a game of skill and should not be played after consuming twelve beers or when you are sitting directly under a fan. The girls are very good at playing this game too. Gambling is strictly illegal in Thailand.

The last game is dominos. The game is played under local rules so get acquainted with them first. As far as I can ascertain, even playing the game of dominos is illegal in Thailand. I assume this is because it is considered to be a gambling game and the authorities realize that most Thais are not going to play the game just for fun. That aside, every bar has a set of dominos. When the girls play among themselves, the domino tiles will be hidden behind the bar, well out of view. If a policeman is nearby, the girls will stop playing and casually pretend to be cleaning down the bar or having a manicure or some other innocuous activity. As soon as PC Plod disappears out of sight, the game continues.

It is different if the girls are playing dominos with a *fa-lung*. Again, as far as I can work out, the police (usually) turn a blind eye if they spot the evil tiles in the hands of a foreigner. Still, no money should be visible or seen to be changing hands (typically, from yours to theirs). Keep all money out of sight at all times.

This is a fictitious story about a fictitious fa-lung who played dominos at a fictitious bar in a fictitious soi and lost 800 baht playing for 20 baht per game. Doing the math, that is a losing streak of forty games! Am I - er - is he a born loser, or was there something more sinister afoot?

These games may all seem a bit childish, but what the hell. You are here on holiday, they are good fun and great 'icebreakers'.

TIP
After you have played a few games with a girl, and if you enjoy her company, it is polite to offer to buy her a drink. After all, she is entertaining you when she possibly could be doing something else. Once you have bought her the drink, she will stay with you as long as you want. Up to you!

TIP
Although gambling is illegal in Thailand, before playing any game with a bar girl for money, make sure that she actually has the money, in the remote possibility that you win. Don't just ask her and wait for her to say "yes". Ask to actually <u>see</u> the cash. A certain fa-lung I know is owed a lot of money from a lot of little angels because I – er, I mean he - did not check their financial status before playing games for money. You know, 20 baht here, 40 baht there. It all adds up. In spite of emphatic promises from award-winning actresses, I have got more chance of winning the Thai lottery than ever collecting the debts. If the fa-lung loses, he must pay up immediately. If <u>she</u> loses, it is on the 'never-never' system.

Massages

You have not lived until you have tried a Thai massage. The genuine ones (ie. no sex) are extremely relaxing and great for all your aches, pains and hangovers. They are relatively inexpensive, starting at around 200 *baht* per hour.

Foot massages are excellent for soothing tired, aching feet and oil massage places are everywhere. Most times, but not all, an oil massage at around 300 *baht* per hour offers the opportunity for an optional 'extra'. The girl will use oil and her hands to relieve your most intimate tensions. If she does not ask for additional money for this service, it is polite to leave her a small tip.

Full body massages are not difficult to find. Once inside, you will be greeted with the sight of up to sixty gorgeous, immaculately dressed, smiling Thai girls sitting on tiered seats behind a glass wall. You can sit at a table or lounge chair, order a drink, relax and watch the ladies as they give you their best 'come on' looks. Any time a girl takes your fancy, simply tell the waiter her number (prominently displayed on their clothing) and she will come out and sit with you. A full body massage will cost you around 600 *baht* for ninety minutes. My friend calls it 'white water rafting' and once you try it you will understand why.

The girl's personal services are extra and negotiable. It will cost upwards of 1,000 *baht*. Never accept her first offer which will be anywhere between 1,500 and 2,000 *baht*. At the time of writing, one establishment offers a 1,500 *baht* all-inclusive arrangement. This is a good deal even though the girl will still try it on for a 'tip'. Condoms are insisted upon.

Other Entertainment

It may surprise you to learn that, apart from the bars, there are other forms of entertainment in Pattaya. When the bars and girls get a bit too much for you, here are some alternatives:

1   Pool & Snooker
     Many bars provide pool tables free of charge for their customers and operate under the 'challenge table' rules. For some bars the cost to play can be anything from 10 to 20 *baht* per game. There are also a number of air conditioned snooker halls throughout the city where quality tables and cues can be found, charging around 100 *baht* per hour. If you can not find an opponent, one of the staff will only be too happy to oblige. Most Thais enjoy playing pool or snooker and some are very good at it.

TIP
Be warned – the surface of some older tables would make
Neil Armstrong feel right at home. Be further warned,
gambling is strictly illegal in Thailand.

2   Thai Boxing

There are several Thai Boxing rings in Pattaya set among nests of Beer Bars. If you like Thai boxing, just sit at any of the bars nearby. The show is free to watch but the drinks are more expensive as each bar contributes to the cost of the shows. When their bout is finished, the boxers disperse into the crowd to solicit tips, almost exclusively from *fa-lung*. Understand that these are exhibition bouts only and are about as genuine as those American TV wrestling shows. To see a genuine Thai Boxing tournament, ask at any tourist agency or look for details of the regular Friday night professional bouts held at the stadium on *Thepprasit* Road.

3   Live Sex Shows

These are illegal and therefore do not exist, but if you stroll along Walking Street in South Pattaya any night of the week, you may be approached by touts advertising the shows. Do not go to any out-of-the-way, dimly-lit, seedy area - especially alone!

Truthfully, I have never been to see one. My philosophy
is; why should I pay to watch someone else have all the
fun. I'd rather put the money towards paying a bar fine
and then star in my own sex show.

4   Cabarets

There are many professional, glitzy, glamorous cabaret and 'lady-man' type shows in Pattaya. These 'extravaganzas' are very professional, have a cover charge and are very popular. It is probably a good idea to book ahead. Throughout Asia, there seems to be a fascination with men dressing up as women and miming songs. It is all in the name of entertainment, I suppose. As well as the larger ones, there are some stages set up in or near the main bar areas that offer cabaret-style entertainment. Most are free to watch but again, the drinks are a little more expensive. These shows are not as professional, but can be fun. Many call for audience participation so, if you are shy, sit up the back.

5   Discos
If you are stone deaf or own a good pair of ear plugs, then you are welcome to go to one of the many discos around the place. Oh, you will also need a large amount of cash. These discos have all the latest high-tech gear, play all the latest mindless noise and charge like there is no tomorrow. There is usually no shortage of ladies present since many freelance girls make the clubs their happy hunting ground. Most discos don't really get thumping and pumping until around midnight.

6   Movies
There are three main cinema complexes in Pattaya. One is in Royal Garden Shopping Centre, referred to as *'loy-en'* by the local Thais. The cost is 80 *baht*. Another is in Big C Shopping Centre opposite *Soi* 2 on Pattaya Second Road. Here, the charge is 80 *baht* weekdays and 90 *baht* on weekends. The newest is in the Alangkarn Complex on Sukhumvit Road at Jomtien. All venues show *fa-lung* movies with subtitles in Thai.

7   Ten Pin Bowling
There is a Ten Pin Bowling Centre in South Pattaya at OD Bowl, one on the third floor of Tops Supermarket in Central Pattaya and another in North Pattaya on Second Road opposite Big C.

8   Go Cart Racing
If you wish to get some realistic driving practice before venturing onto Pattaya's streets, there are two Go Cart Speedway circuits on *Thepprasit* Road Jomtien and one off *Sukhumvit* Road North Pattaya.

9   Shooting, Fishing, Scuba Diving, Water Skiing, Sky Diving, Golf. Not interested, don't know, don't care. Ask around for the best places and the best deals.

CHAPTER

5

The Bar Girls

*"What's a nice girl like you
doing in a place like this?"*

In spite of emphatic denials, the main attraction that many men find in Pattaya is the girls. I can not decide what it is about them that makes them so appealing and attractive. They are fun-loving, friendly, happy and have exterior physical beauty, but they also have inner qualities that seem to strike at the very heart of foreign men. It would take a man of stone not to fall in love several times a day. It is not just their eyes or their smile, but the way that they can say the right thing at the right time and turn a grown man to putty. I have seen naked Go Go dancers on stage who could give you such a look that would have you believe they were as pure and innocent as the driven snow.

They are a paradox. On the one hand they will talk freely and openly about sex and the most intimate details of their lives yet, in the privacy of a bedroom, dress and undress with a towel around them because they are shy. Even the girls who work in Go Go bars and display all or 99% of their bodies to ogling customers can be shy in the bedroom. On the one hand they will tell you that they do not like lies, do not tell lies or like people who do and in the next breath come out with the biggest load of garbage that you've ever heard. On the one hand they will tell you they don't like 'butterflies' and next week go with seven different men in as many days.

They are experts at making tourists feel welcome and men feel like kings. If Hollywood ever runs short of actresses, they should send their talent scouts to Pattaya.

My last girlfriend had a roommate, Lek, who had a boyfriend, John. Lek worked bar but I was told that she did not go with fa-lung because she was waiting for John to return. I eventually met John and the four of us had a great time together. One night, John and I went on a bar crawl and finished up at a bar where he became enamoured with a cute bar girl. At 2:00am I left John in the arms of the latest object of his desire. His intention was to go 'short-time' with her and then see Lek in a couple of hours.

Back at the apartment, I was confronted by Lek who asked where John was. Of course I lied, saying that he was with some fa-lung friends and would be back soon.

In the early morning, I was awakened by the sound of Lek crying. She was sitting on the floor looking at her photo of John and sobbing uncontrollably. I felt so sorry for her. When John finally crawled back at about 7:00am, he managed to explain (lie) his way out of it.

The twist to this story is, after John left, I found out that Lek had another boyfriend, an American, who was arriving a few days later. Both John and the American were sending her money. My girlfriend had lied to me and Lek had put on an Academy Award winning performance for my benefit.

The girls take pride in their appearance and usually wear the most attractive and the neatest clothing that their finances will allow. This is in contrast to the *fa-lung* who, while roaming the streets of Thailand, appear to dress according to whatever yardage of scrap curtain material they can fit around their robust waistlines.

TIP

Here's a fashion tip: Wearing socks with sandals or open-toed shoes is to fashion what a turd sandwich is to cordon bleu.

It does not matter if a man is facially-challenged, over fifty years of age and has a beer gut that starts from the neck. He does not have to be a young movie star to attract the attention of one of the bar girls. If the Elephant Man mated with The Hunchback of Notre Dame, the ugliest of their male offspring could get a girlfriend here, providing he had money. The bar girls appear not to care so much about physical appearance or age when it comes to *fa-lung*. Many girls have told me (and I believe them), that they prefer to go with older men. I can only presume that this is because an older man is likely to have more money and is generally not as demanding in the bedroom.

To the girls, working in a bar and 'going with' a *fa-lung* is just a job. Just as we go to work each day in our own country, these girls go to work in a bar. At the end of their eight to twelve hour shift, they are tired, usually hungry and just want to relax and forget about work, the trouble with the boss or the rude customers.

Many girls take to bar work like a duck to water but most would much rather be living with their family or husband and working at a 'respectable' job. So why did she come to work in a bar? The answer is universal and blatantly obvious. For m-o-n-e-y. There is no other reason. And working in a bar has its advantages. It is not difficult nor does it require any particular skill or educational qualification. She has the opportunity to earn a lot of money, to sleep most of the day and, if she is so inclined, to party most of the night. She has not been sold into 'sexual slavery' nor has she been forced at gunpoint to work in the bars. Although this type of abomination does exist in Asia, it is usually contained in remote areas away from the eyes of the foreign press. It is certainly not prevalent in bars catering to foreigners. A bar girl is free to quit at any time but, if she chooses to stay, it is because the economic benefits are greater than anything on offer in her village in the province.

TIP

Never forget your place in the bar girl's order of importance. It goes as follows and, apart from numbers 5 through 8 which can change depending on her personal circumstances, the order never varies.

1   MONEY

2   GOLD

3   FOOD

4   SLEEPING

5   CHILD/CHILDREN

6   GRANDPARENTS, MOTHER, FATHER

7   THAI HUSBAND OR BOYFRIEND, SIBLINGS AND OTHER FAMILY MEMBERS

8   THAI FRIENDS

9   EVERY OTHER THAI PERSON IN THE WORLD, DOWN TO THE LOWLIEST BANGKOK BEGGAR

10   THE FAMILY BUFFALO   (HEALTHY OR OTHERWISE)

11   PET DOG, CAT OR RAT

12   THE FLEAS ON PET DOG, CAT OR RAT

13   YOU

Whenever a choice has to be made between any of the above groups, the Thai girl will always choose from the top down. Many a foreign male has deluded himself into thinking that his importance to the lady is higher than it really is. When push comes to shove, he has been sadly mistaken.

Life of a Bar Girl

*"Before you criticize someone, walk a mile in their shoes.
That way, if they get angry, you are a mile away and
you have their shoes!"*

There is no girl working in the bars of Thailand who is not supporting or helping to support at least one other person. They are mostly upcountry girls from poor rural communities who chose the world's oldest profession because they saw it as their best chance of improving the financial lot of themselves and their families. Almost every bar girl I have spoken to has at least one child. In many cases the father was a Thai boyfriend who got her pregnant and then (in almost every case), shot through. Most of the girls have had their heart broken by a Thai man. The girl's mother, friends or relatives in the province will be taking care of the child. The girl is working in a bar to earn money to send home to support her family and child. The Thai boyfriend who did a runner does not (usually) support the child financially.

Do her parents know what she does for a living? Probably. Do they care? Probably not. The economic benefits to the family far outweigh any moral concerns. With or without a child, she will be sending money home to care for her family. If she has a good month and meets one or two kind (generous) *fa-lung*, after paying the rent and other bills, money is sent home. If she has an ordinary month, surviving only on wages and tips, then no money is sent home.

She may also be supporting her Thai boyfriend. In spite of what they may tell you, many of the girls still have a Thai boyfriend or even a husband. (The consensus among expats is around 80%.) They usually do not keep their activities a secret from him either. In many cases, not only does the Thai guy know about her profession, but more often than not, he encourages it.

Most of the bar girls live in apartments that they share with up to four other girls. The monthly rent will be from 2,000 to 3,000 *baht*, plus another 300 to 500 *baht* for electricity and water. Therefore, each girl sharing the room is up for around 1,000 *baht* per month for accommodation.

She will also spend around 60 *baht* per day on food (Thai food is not expensive if you know where to go and many of the bars provide free meals for their girls). This means that her cost of living is around 3,000 *baht* per month. In an average month, the wages from the bar plus tips, a girl could cover this amount. In low season, maybe not. In high season, this is not much of a problem. However, this does not leave enough money to save or to send home. The only way a girl can send money home is to find a generous *fa-lung*.

Wages from the bars vary greatly but if the girl works for the full month she may receive, for example 2,500 *baht*. Each day, the tips received from customers are divided up among all the girls who worked that shift. If a customer buys a girl a drink, she receives a commission.

TIP
If a particular girl was very good to you and you want to show your appreciation, but only to her, when you 'check bin' place the tip directly into her hand. Any money left on the little silver tray is divided among all the girls, but she can keep money that you give to her directly.

TIP
When you ask a girl if she would like a drink, she may say 'num som' (orange juice). It could be that she does not drink alcohol, but don't get the idea that she is doing you any favours by ordering something cheap. It is simply that the commission she receives on orange juice is more than she gets from ordering say, a marguerita. She will get maybe 30 baht from the 'num som' but only 20 baht from an alcoholic drink.

If she elects to 'go' with a *fa-lung*, he will pay the bar fine which in most Beer Bars is 200 *baht*. The girl will receive around 50 *baht* from this. Whatever money the girl receives from him after that is hers. If, for whatever reason, she does not want to work one night, she must pay her own bar fine. If she goes with the same *fa-lung* for more than one night, he must pay the bar fine for each night he is with her although there are cases when this does not apply. Some girls, 'freelancers', are not on 'salary' but merely work for tips, drinks and the prospect of meeting a generous *fa-lung*. He will probably have to pay the bar fine for the first night but, after that, it may not be required.

When she cannot cover her rent, the girl can sometimes borrow money from the bar or her friends who have had better luck. If all else fails, then there are characters who visit the bars and discreetly loan the girls money. This works on the Chinese '6 for 5' system. I loan you 5 and at the end of the month you pay back 6. The guy will lend the girl 1,000 *baht* and every day for the next 30 days she will pay back 40 *baht*. If she misses one payment, the next night she has to pay back 80 *baht*. At the end of 30 days, any outstanding balance becomes the '5' and she then owes 120% of that amount. The complexities of compound interest have not sunk into the average bar girl. When your stomach is empty and you have no money, it does not seem to matter.

Some girls make an absolute fortune by accumulating a stable of generous boyfriends and some could be described as being totally greedy, selfish and cunning to the point of evil. They want it all and don't care how they get it or who they hurt in the process. But the vast majority is not like that. Most simply make a sustainable living. At least it is more money than they could earn selling chewing gum back home in the province.

At a bar one night I saw a girl that I had never seen before. She looked very young and so I asked another lady how old the girl was. The reply was "Sixteen." With a display of moral indignation, I responded that she was too young to be working in a bar. Further, I asked, "What would her mother say if she knew that her daughter was working in a bar?" With a straight face she replied, "Why don't you ask her? That is her mother standing next to her."

Freelancers

Some girls who appear to be working in a bar are not on salary but operate as 'freelancers'. These girls come and go as they please and usually have a few favourite bars to hang out in. If one bar has no customers, they move on to another. Many freelancers are migratory - they will work in Pattaya during the high season then Bangkok or Chiang Mai for the rest of the year because there is less of a low season in those places.

A bar fine is usually payable to take her out of the bar and 'lady drink' prices are usually charged for her drinks but this should be a 'one off' and only payable for the first night. After that, it is up to her whether she goes back to the bar or not.

Some freelance operators do not attach themselves to any bar but hang around places frequented by *fa-lung* in the hope of attracting the attention and affection of one. They can be found in discos, nightclubs and coffee shops or walking or sitting along Beach Road, especially towards the South Pattaya end. The benefit of going with one of these freelancers is that you don't have to pay a bar fine or pay for lady drinks. Unfortunately, there is also a down side:

1   Never go to her room for your intimate encounter. Some *fa-lung* have done this only to discover, too late, that they were not alone in the room. Her boyfriend or accomplice was hiding and waiting to accost or rifle through the wallet of the unsuspecting visitor while he was otherwise occupied. Some *fa-lung* have accepted a drink offered by their new friend only to wake up the next morning with a severe headache, no money, no clothes and no sign of the girl. They were lucky – at least they woke up.

2   Some freelance girls are not really 'girls' at all, but *katoeys* or 'lady-men'. It is dark, they are beautiful, you are drunk and by the time you get back to your room and find out the truth, it is too late. In many cases it will cost you money just to get rid of her/him.

3   If anything unfortunate does happen to you, you have no recourse. What are you going to tell the police? "Yes officer, her name was *Lek*, she was short, had black hair, brown eyes, was wearing blue jeans and I met her on Beach Road." The police will laugh you out of their office faster than you can say "Stupid *fa-lung*". Another twist was reported in the *Pattaya Mail* February 2004:

At around 2:00am police were called to an apartment building after hotel staff reported an incident. Officers arrived at the room to find a Thai woman crying with a foreigner standing nearby. The woman pointed to him saying that he had raped her. Both were taken to Soi 9 Police Station for questioning. The man told police he was walking along Beach Road when he met the woman. They sat, chatted and agreed on a price for services before going back to his room. Once their activities were finished, he paid the agreed rate but the woman demanded more. He refused and tried to remove her from the room, at which time she began screaming.

Her side of the story was that she was sitting on the beachfront when the man approached her. They chatted and he asked her to go back to his room for a massage for 300 baht. She alleged, during the massage, the foreigner became amorous and forced her to have sex. Afterwards he released her and tried to kick her out of the room, at which time she called for help.

Police recorded the statements and the woman was sent to a hospital for medical examination as proof of the allegations. She returned to the station to proceed with her claims. The man asked police if he could settle the matter with the woman and they came to an agreement of 4,500 baht. Officers then released the pair on their own accord.

Be careful!

Language of a Bar Girl

Thai is a tonal language. Words are spoken with a high tone, mid tone, low tone, falling tone or rising tone. You may also know that the Thai word *fa-lung* is not a derogatory term. Literally, it means foreigner, Westerner, European or basically, any non-Thai. Don't get upset when you are constantly called a *'fa-lung'*.

Now, what you probably don't know is that, in an attempt to express their true opinion of you as a foreigner, the bar girls add the English adjective 'Stupid' before the noun *'fa-lung'*. (This is contrary to Thai grammar which states that you should always place the adjective after the noun.) They give the word 'Stupid' a low tone - a very low tone. So low, in fact, that most of the time it is inaudible. Never forget, whether you hear it or not, your title is always "Stupid *fa-lung*".

In the language of bar girls, there are three given truths to be aware of:

1   All girls working in the bar only ever work as 'cashier'.

      Question: *How do you confuse a bar girl?*
      Answer: *Write a letter to a bar and address it simply to the 'Cashier'.*
      Question: *How do you create havoc at a bar?*
      Answer: *Address the envelope as above but make the enclosed letter as vague and brief as possible. Mention that you want her to e-mail you her bank account details so that you can send her 10,000 baht to help out with her 'problem'. If that doesn't start World War III in the bar, nothing will!*

2   No bar girl ever has sex with a customer. If a *fa-lung* pays her bar fine and she 'goes' with him, it is only to sleep - no *boomsing*.

3   Every girl working in the bar has a 'problem' at home that can be easily solved by a substantial injection of your money.

"I never go with *fa-lung* before.
I work cashier."

Ok, so they may not strictly be 'truths', but this is Pattaya and truth is in short supply. There are t-shirts with the top ten or twenty most common lies told to *fa-lung* by bar girls compiled on the back. These lists are by no means complete.

For example, you return to a bar to see a girl that you had been with on a previous occasion. She is not there and you are told, "She go room. Have stomach ache," or maybe, "She have to go home. Mama have problem." This, of course, is total bullshit. She has actually gone with another *fa-lung*. You got there too late. Thai food must not be very good for you going by the number of bar girls who get stomach aches. You will never get the truth out of any of her friends at the bar, so don't bother pressing the subject. When (or if) you see her again, she will stick to the same story. Remember the one-legged chicken?

He had only been in Pattaya for four days and had been with the same girl since the night he arrived. He told me that everything was great, she was great, the world was great, etc. He went on to say that he was going to be on his own for a couple of days because Lek had to go home for Christmas. I felt obliged to tell him that there was a possibility (in my mind a 100% certainty) that she may not be telling the truth. I explained that Thais do not celebrate Christmas and it was possible that she had another fa-lung, a regular boyfriend, coming to Pattaya over that time. He responded confidently "No. I'm sure that she's sincere."

Two nights later I ran into him while he was walking around by himself and invited him to join me at a bar in Naklua. Guess who we found sitting lovingly with another fa-lung at one of the bars nearby? My friend meekly said "Hello" to her as we passed.
"I did warn you," I told him.
He replied, "I know, but she seemed so genuine!"
They all do.

MONEY *Still* NUMBER ONE

Money Number One! No bar girl is going to give up the money she could get from you for any other reason than the possibility she will get more money from someone else. If she can keep you 'on hold' for a while, all the better. Many girls become very skilled at juggling boyfriends and there are stories attesting to this. My favourite is the one about the girl who went with one boyfriend to the airport and tearfully waved him goodbye from the departure area then headed straight to the arrivals section to meet her other boyfriend due to arrive an hour later. Was it luck or unbelievable organizational skills?

One common English expression used by the ladies of the bars is "Up to you". Along with, "Hello sexy man", "Sit down please" and "What you like some drink?" it must be one of the first English phrases they learn. Although indicating that you are in the position of power, it can become annoying when you are continually given "Up to you" as the response to questions to which you genuinely would like her opinion or suggestion.

"Where would you like to go?"	"Up to you."
"How much money do you want?"	"Up to you."
"What is your name?"	"Up to you."

My personal favourite is the story of the starry-eyed fa-lung who asked his bar girl companion, "Do you really love me?"
Without hesitation she replied, "Up to you!"

But, all jokes aside, the basic premise is absolutely true. It *is* up to you. Americans put it another way – "It's your dime". Never forget that *you* are the one who is paying to be entertained, not the other way round.

I made many costly mistakes when I forgot this important point. I found that I was paying a small fortune to do something I did not want to do with someone I really did not want to be with. Stupid fa-lung!

Bar Girl v *Fa-lung*

Imagine if you will that you are about to go to war, a war in which you believe you have the advantage. You have all the firepower, the education, the experience and such a variety of choices that you should win hands down. Further imagine that you go into this war cocksure and confident of victory only to find that the enemy has one or two tricks up their sleeve that you were unaware of. The enemy is a lot smarter than you gave them credit for and they have at their disposal an arsenal of weapons that you could not have imagined. What you thought would be an easy victory turns out to be a war of attrition and you eventually find yourself out of ammunition and with your back to the wall.

No, I'm not talking about the Americans in Vietnam nor the Russians in Afghanistan, but about the only war that really matters – the battle of the sexes. In particular, the battle of wits that is fought every day in thousands of bars throughout Thailand – Bar girl v *Fa-lung*. Each day, *fa-lung* arrive in this wonderful country with pockets full of money and heads full of the wrong attitude. Those who come believing that with their spending power and the availability of women, they have such an advantage they can not lose, go home scratching their heads wondering where it all went. Sure they had a great time but, in a place where almost everything is cheaper than in their own country, "How did I end up spending so much money?"

The answer is simple. They underestimated the intelligence and resolve of the enemy, specifically, the bar girls. It is all one big mind game which the girls are so good at that most *fa-lung* don't even know they have been playing until it is all over.

Modern warfare, bar girl style, consists of four distinct waves - The Bait, The Intelligence Gathering, The Reassurance and The Flattery. There are no Rules of Engagement, no Geneva Conventions and no prisoners. It is impossible to know all the tricks but, in each encounter, she uses her most lethal weapons, her cheeky smile and her sweet mouth. The fun begins the moment he steps outside the sanctuary of his hotel.

87

"Hello sexy man!"

First Wave – The Bait

Thai bar girls soon come to realize that foreign men find them attractive. The ones with darker skin learn that foreign men find them more attractive than Thai men who are drawn to girls with lighter skin tones. All she has to do is keep clean, dress to the best her finances will allow and dab on a bit of war paint from time to time. The problem is, because men find so many of them attractive, the competition in the bars is fierce. The smarter girls quickly pick up a few key words of English and learn to take full advantage of their beautiful smile and seductive eyes.

Once she casts her eye upon an unsuspecting target, her sweet mouth fires the first Exocet of the battle and directs it towards every man's Achilles' Heel, his ego. It comes in the form of the classic, "Hello sexy man." I have doubts whether any of them know what it means or the full ramifications of the statement, but what they do know is that it is a winner, a tried and true moneyspinner. The beauty of her not understanding the words means she can keep a straight face while saying them.

It comes as a shock to the male system to be continually told by beautiful young women that he is a sexy man. The danger for the *falung* is that, if he is told the same lie often enough, he may start to believe it. Maybe all the females with 20-20 vision back home are wrong. Maybe the mirrors are distorted and his doctors are jealous of the way he has kept in shape over the years. "Hey, maybe I am a sexy man – a three hundred pound, old, bald, genuinely sexy man!"

I have an antidote though. Each night before I go out, I shower and stand naked in front of a full-length mirror, repeating aloud, "The females in your own country, the mirrors and the doctors who told you that they have never seen a body like yours outside a jar of formaldehyde are correct. You are truly ugly. The only reason that you are even remotely appealing is that you portray an image of wealth. You are disgusting but look like you have money." This medicine, although painful to swallow, is usually good for twenty-four hours.

Second Wave – Intelligence Gathering

Knowledge is power so, to gain the advantage, combatants need to collect as much information about their adversary as possible. After initial pleasantries are exchanged between the *fa-lung* and the hostess designated to be his inquisitor, he will be asked his name, what country he comes from and how long he is staying. It is easy to believe that this is simply polite conversation, but there is a sinister purpose to these questions.

> *Sitting with a friend one night, he inquired "Why is she asking me all these questions?" I replied that she was merely gathering intelligence. "Good. It looks like she could certainly use some." Alas, he was an empty MasterCard just waiting to happen.*

His name is required for identification and along with his nationality, forms a unique bar code for future reference. He is John-from-England or Peter-from-America or Hans-from-Germany and each girl will then know who the other girls are talking about.

His nationality is also required for currency conversion. Should he be short of *baht* and pay the girl in dollars, pounds or euros, she has to know the exchange rate to calculate what she is getting and more importantly, if she is being short-changed.

"How long are you staying?" comes as part of a trilogy of related questions. "This your first time Thailand?" and "How long have you been here?" being the other two. General interest questions? Yes. Innocuous? No.

If it is his first time in Thailand he is neither street-wise nor bar-wise and he is easy game for a clever bar girl. If he has been here for only one or two days, then he still has plenty of money to spend and if he is staying for another week or so, she has plenty of time to get it. He is a Class A Golden Goose, the most sought after prey for any bar girl and she will fight tooth and nail to get and hold his attention.

At the bottom of the scale is the Class Z Waste Of Time. He is the bar-wise *fa-lung* who has been to Thailand many times, has stayed here for a long time and has no intention of leaving. (Note: 'wise' is a relative term and in this context merely means 'wiser than totally stupid'.) This guy, if he actually tells the truth, is given short shrift by the girls and is looked upon with disdain for taking up a valuable seat which could otherwise be occupied by a Class A, B or C *fa-lung*. This guy, however, very rarely tells the truth and so the girls have to look for more subtle signs before they can relegate him to the Bar Twilight Zone with the beggars, lepers, *fa-lung* with no money and other undesirables.

Half way down the ladder is the Class M *Hah-sip Hah-sip*. You can figure out for yourself what half way between Class A and Class Z is, but a bar girl will have to ask further questions before determining if he is a bankable commodity. Since it is not his first time in Thailand, the first is whether or not he already has a Thai wife or girlfriend. The second is whether he can speak Thai. An answer in the affirmative to either of these questions and he immediately slides to Class Z. A negative response means that she must use other methods of assessment.

Not all the intelligence gathering is verbal. Thai girls are the best I have ever seen at reading body language and picking up subtle signs as to a person's character. Within thirty minutes, the more experienced ones will know approximately how much money he has, what pocket he keeps it in, whether he is a cheap Charlie or a spendthrift and how much he would be likely to part with for her company for an evening.

Once the interrogation and evaluation is complete, he can be tagged and pigeonholed. Now it is up to each individual girl to decide how much effort she will put in to earn his favour. This is where it gets interesting because she has calculated her potential rewards, she knows how much ammunition she is willing to expend and so she plans the next wave of her attack. It comes in the form of reassuring comments about herself.

Third Wave – The Reassurance

The bar girls have this down to a fine art. In amongst the bamboo English there are the standard lines. I often wonder where they get this stuff because they are always the same lines, word for word, and each comes in almost identical order. Is there a book for bar girls listing all the lines that can be spun to gullible *fa-lung*? Maybe there is a secret school in some out of the way *soi* where they teach it. In any event, once they have him seated with his drink order on the way the bullshit will run thicker than treacle.

The first and my personal favourite is the, "I no like work bar" line. This is sometimes coupled with, "I only work bar one month." The fact that she has been working in bars for five years and only worked at this particular bar for one month is inconsequential. The idea is to give you the impression that she is not really like the rest of them. She is not really a bar girl. She may reinforce the point by actually saying, "I not same lady bar." Some time ago, the girls used to add the line "I only work cashier," to this barrage of bullshit but I get the impression that they finally realized that *fa-lung* were not as stupid as they looked. Even the most myopic *fa-lung* correctly concluded that there were not ten thousand cashiers employed in the bars of Pattaya.

Most girls are also aware that foreign men have a deep distrust of Thai men, whether it is warranted or not. She must now attempt to distance herself from Thai men and ingratiate herself with the foreigner. "I no like Thai man," is the wording and it will come out in any general conversation regarding past or present boyfriends. Every bar girl will tell you the same thing. In fact, the majority of them (the consensus among expats is around 80%) have a Thai boyfriend, lover or husband. Thailand did not become the most ethnically pure nation in South East Asia because the female population could not stand the male population.

By the end of this wave of her attack, if he is still seated at the bar, she has assured him that she really is a nice girl who has been forced to do something that she does not want to do through temporary economic necessity.

The Final Assault – The Flattery

Convincing him that she really is a wonderful person is not quite enough. She now has to convince him that she does really, truly, cross-my-heart-and-hope-to-die like him. The nature of a male is such that his ego or conscience will make it difficult for him to dislike any female who professes that she likes him and is attracted to him. She knows this and she uses it to her advantage.

> *"The reason that adulation is not displeasing is that, though untrue, it shows one to be of consequence enough, in one way or other, to induce people to lie."*
>
> Lord Byron (1788–1824), English poet.

If he is young, say under thirty, she will begin with, "I like young man. No like old man." If he is older than dirt he will hear, "I like old man. No like young man." If he initially told her he was from America, "I like man America. No like man England." If he is from the UK, "I like man England. No like man America." If he is fat, she will respond with, "I like man *poong ploo-ee*." She may go even further and point to her own 45kg frame and declare that she too is *poong ploo-ee*.

If his complexion is snow white, she will tell him how much she likes white. She will point out how black her own skin is and express her desire to be white like him. If he is as bald as a billiard ball, covered in tattoos, has earrings, nose-rings, missing teeth and wears horned-rimmed glasses, she will remark how much she likes each of these features and sum up by insisting that the overall combination makes him one hell of an attractive man.

With that, the battle has been waged and it is simply a matter of waiting for the result. There is no necessity to contemplate what makes the *fa-lung* the victor because such an outcome is beyond the realms of possibility. The best he can hope for is a draw. The girl, on the other hand, claims outright victory immediately the *fa-lung* raises the white flag by asking that immortal question: "How much is your bar fine?"

ESSENTIAL THAI – ENGLISH FOR THE BARS

If she says …	**She REALLY means …**
Hello sexy man.	Hello stupid *fa-lung*.
Hello. Sit down please.	Hello. Come in sucker.
You very handsome/sexy man.	You look like you have a lot of money.
Where you come from?	What currency do I need to check the exchange rate?
Your first time Thailand?	Just how gullible are you?
I no have fa-lung. Fa-lung no like me.	I have many *fa-lung*. Going for your sympathy vote works every time.
How long you stay Thailand?	How long have I got to bleed you dry?
Which hotel you stay?	Where will I be sleeping tonight?
You want play game?	Buy me a drink, dickhead.
You have Thai lady?	Do I have to share your money with anyone else?
I no like Thai man. *or* *I no have Thai boyfriend.*	I have a Thai boyfriend and all the money I make I use to support him.

I love you.	I love your money.
You have good heart.	You have a big wallet.
You good man for me.	You are spending a lot of money. You are good for my bank account.
I miss you.	I miss your money.
I no want money.	I want your money.
I no want money. Only want you.	I want all your money.
I go with you for free.	This will cost you double.
I no butterfly.	I only sleep with my boyfriend and any *fa-lung* who pays my bar fine.
I no like work bar.	Working bar is easier than picking rice or chili in the province. More money too.
I only work cashier.	I am a liar.
I go with him before, but no boomsing.	I truly am a liar.
I not lie. I no like go-hok.	I am a BIG liar.
She same same my sister.	I met her for the first time last night.
I wait for you till you come back Thailand.	I will wait until you are securely on the plane home.

MONEY *Still* NUMBER ONE

My friend me.	My boyfriend.
My friend you.	Your friend.
Money me.	My money.
Money you.	My money.
We go to XYZ Bar tonight?	I owe drinks to some friends at XYZ Bar. You can pay.
I need 4,000 baht to give my Mama for...	My boyfriend needs new tires for his motorcycle.
You give me 10,000 baht now and I stay with you for two weeks.	You give me 10,000 baht now and you will never see me or the money again.
I never cheat.	When you look, I never cheat. When you don't look, I cheat.
You can not come my apartment. It not clean.	You can not come to my apartment because my boyfriend is there sleeping off a hangover.
Money Number One!	Money Number One!

General Advice

"Remember, no matter how good she looks, some other guy is sick and tired of putting up with her shit!"

Experience is the best teacher and this is particularly true of Thailand. In fact, here experience is the only teacher and all the advice under the sun is meaningless without it. For what it is worth, the following notes may help you save money while traversing the cultural minefield that is Thailand and gaining that much-needed experience.

1   Thais in general, and bar girls in particular, like to have fun. *Sanook sanook.* They like to laugh, play games, joke, kid around and be happy and tend to avoid the company of people who are sad or miserable. If you are seen to be a 'fun' person they will be attracted to you and want to be with you. If you treat them well and they enjoy being with you, they will repay you by taking genuine care of you while not attempting to extract extra money from you at every opportunity. Treat every girl you are with, whether it be for one hour or one year, as if she were your one and only girlfriend. Show her kindness and respect and you will be repaid in kind. This is not to say that you should let your guard down but you will have a lot more fun.

97

2　　Once you have decided to go with a particular girl, ask her if she wants to go with you. If she agrees, pay the bar fine and *check bin* immediately. Do not stay at that bar and do not come back later with her. Even if the night is still young and you do not wish to return to your room, leave that bar and go to another one not too close. The reasons for this are twofold:

a) While you have been buying drinks for the girl of your dreams, before you paid the bar fine, she receives a commission on each 'lady drink'. Her drinks are more expensive than if you had brought the same drink for yourself. After you pay the bar fine, theoretically her working day at that bar is over and she becomes a customer, not an employee. Therefore her drinks should be the normal price. This does not always happen and some girls will want to keep you at the bar, still filling your *bin* with the purple slips of paper and collecting their commission. By going to another bar you can avoid this added expense.

b) As mentioned earlier, the girls in the bars form a type of sorority. Your angel may share a room with some of the others. As a 'sisterhood', they help each other out in times of need. Your girl may even owe a few favours. Once it is seen that she has caught herself a *fa-lung*, these favours may be politely called in (you won't understand because the conversation will be in Thai). All you will hear from your delightful companion is, "You buy my friend a drink? She have no money." You will be surprised at how many 'friends' she has that all suddenly pop over to say hello. I have been caught many times with this trick. It can get expensive.

__TIP__
Instead of buying lady drinks all night, buy the first one for the apple of your eye and quietly tell her that if she stays with you and does not ask you for another drink all night, you will give her 100 baht tip when you check bin. She will enthusiastically agree. Later, whether you pay the bar fine for her or not, keep your promise.

3   Once you have been with a girl from a particular bar and for whatever reason have decided that you do not wish to go with her again, it is considered bad manners to return to that bar and select another girl. Your first girl will lose face in front of her friends and your second choice will be put off by the fact that you did not pick her in the first place. Choose carefully the first time. One way out of it is, if on your next trip to the bar, your original choice has already gone with, or is busy with, another *fa-lung*. It is then OK to select another girl and nobody loses face. Of course, you now have a problem if you go back a third time to find both girls available. How do you get out of it? You tell me and we'll both know. My only advice is to make sure neither girl loses face in front of her friends.

A friend has a novel way around this. He systematically bar fines every girl in the bar. His reputation as a 'butterfly' is thus entrenched in stone with all the girls understanding he is not looking for a meaningful relationship. His social standing is one notch above pond scum. If you do this, make sure you give each girl the same amount of money because playing favourites will quickly get you into trouble.

4   When you are with your girl, do not go to a bar, shop or restaurant of her choosing. If she says "We go here," then go somewhere else. More often than not, she will have friends or relatives at that particular establishment and she will be eager to repay outstanding favours or debts with your money. Either that or she may be getting a commission from your purchases. This is not always the case and some girls do genuinely look after you when it comes to saving you from being overcharged by retailers. However, in the beginning, at least until you are familiar with the place, it is better to be safe than sorry.

5   Do not get sucked into buying flowers for the new love of your life. Buying flowers for your *fa-lung* wife or girlfriend is a wonderful romantic gesture and she may go weak at the knees

"When I say you buy me five *baht* gold,
I not mean you give me five *baht*!"

with such a thoughtful loving gift. Thai bar girls could not care less about receiving flowers and one even told me, in all seriousness, "I can not eat flowers." Receiving a bunch of flowers from you evokes the same feeling that you get when someone buys you a pair of socks or a handkerchief for your birthday. Don't waste your money. Buying her one of those cuddly stuffed toys is almost as bad. I have seen many Thai girl's apartments filled with a veritable zoo of stuffed animals of all shapes, sizes and colours and not one of the girls could tell me who gave her what.

6   If you wish to give the object of your devotion a gift, the only things that Thai bar girls truly appreciate are money (Number One) and gold. Pure 24k gold or Thai gold (22k) only - none of that 18k or gold-plated rubbish. The gold they want comes in the form of a necklace, chain, bracelet or ring. It is sold by weight and in Thailand the unit of weight is called a '*baht*'. This is not to be confused with the Thai currency which is also called a '*baht*'. One '*baht*' of gold weighs around 15 grams and will cost you somewhere between 6,000 and 7,000 *baht* in Thai currency, depending on the current world price of gold. The gold you buy for her is her 'safety net'. If ever she is desperate for money she can always sell or pawn it.

I remember buying my first gold chain. My girlfriend picked it out after much deliberation and was truly delighted as we headed for the door with her new adornment hanging triumphantly from her gorgeous neck. I should have twigged when the gold shop owner farewelled me with "See you again soon," as I hurried out the door. Over the next twelve months I ended up buying that same gold chain three times.

Gold is also a status symbol. By flaunting her gold jewellery, the other girls will know that she has a kind and generous *fa-lung* taking care of her. *Jai dee!* She has moved up a rung on the bar girl's social ladder.

I bought my girlfriend a beautiful dress ring for her birthday. That evening when we went out to dinner, I was surprised to see that she was not wearing the ring. She made some feeble excuse but later she questioned me regarding the 'silver' appearance of the metal in the ring. The penny dropped. She did not wear the ring because she thought it was silver. I explained to her that it was not silver but in fact 'white gold' or a platinum/gold alloy which was much more expensive than gold. (In truth, I confess that it was probably galvanized iron or tin, going by what I paid for it in a Hong Kong street market). Her greedy little eyes lit up and she reached into her purse, pulled out the ring and slipped it on her delicate finger. My girl and I have since split up under, shall we say, not the best of circumstances. One of the few little pleasures I have in life is picturing the little darling trying to convince a Thai gold shop owner that her ring was very expensive platinum when she tried to sell it five minutes after we parted company.

7   The only other gift that a Thai girl may appreciate is clothes, especially shoes. It appears there is a little Imelda Marcos in all women. Don't initiate the purchase yourself. Let her see something she really likes and then, if you are feeling exceptionally loving or benevolent, offer to buy it for her. Be careful. You will have then set a precedent and thereafter, every time she sees something she likes, your hand (or hers) will be reaching for your wallet. Let it be known that your gift is a one-off for something special and not a daily event. If you have limited finances, avoid buying from the big tourist-oriented shopping centres. Inexpensive clothing can be purchased from the markets. In Pattaya, two you should consider are the *Soi* Buakow day market on Tuesday and Friday and the Thepprasit Road night market on the weekend.

8   One last comment on gift giving. When you give a Thai - any Thai - a present that is giftwrapped do not expect them to open it

then and there in front of you. Thai custom is to put the present aside and open it later when they are alone. This way, they can avoid an obvious display of disappointment if the gift turns out to be something they less than appreciate.

9   When taking a Thai girl out for a meal it is easy and convenient to allow her to order for the both of you. Big mistake! She will always order too much food. Perhaps it is because, for most of the time she can only afford to eat such meagre meals, now that she has money (you) she is going to make up for it in a big way. You will end up with your table covered with six to ten dishes of delicious food that has hardly been touched, your girlfriend lounging back patting her stomach and saying, "*Im*" [I am full].

TIP
A good trick, if you are going to allow her to order, is to tell her beforehand that you are not very hungry, even if you are starving. She will probably only order one dish for you plus six or seven for herself. After she has taken one mouthful from each dish and declared that she is "im", you can then safely eat the rest of the food on the table. Be careful though. Don't show your hand too early or she will do another round of ordering for you.

10   Being a man of the world, you probably realize by now that women are strange animals indeed. Women can be very moody and temperamental at times. Thai girls are no exception. In fact, they are the worst. They can change moods in an instant, without provocation and definitely without warning. I mean a full 180° turnaround.

Hell hath no fury like a pissed-off Thai girl. Forget all about *jai yen yen*. Initially, they become very vocal. Thankfully you will not understand a word as they rattle off abuse in machinegun Thai. Next, they become very physical and very destructive. Once you have picked a Thai girl's mood changing for the worse, remove from her presence, or remove her from the presence of,

... to allow the girl to order for both of you.
Big mistake!

all sharp or heavy objects. Follow this by distancing her from anything that belongs to you. The objects on which she vents her spleen will belong to you, not to her. The girls become irrational, not stupid.

My friend made the mistake of walking out of his apartment once he realized that his girlfriend was in a severely agitated state. He returned later to find that his normally docile mate had used his golf clubs to obliterate his TV and stereo system. Then, for good measure, she had destroyed his golf clubs.

Once you have ensured the safety of your personal property, distance yourself from her and give her time to cool down. There is nothing to be gained by staying around and arguing with her. (Refer Chapter 3, Lesson Four – Reasoning and Logic) With nobody to rant and rave at, her mood may change back to normal just as quickly as it went off the rails. The fun part is that you will probably never know what you did wrong in the first place.

11 If you are 100% heterosexual there is an extra precaution you should take. Thailand has its share of *katoeys* ('lady men', transsexuals or transvestites) and some of them are incredibly beautiful. Follow this rule: If you suspect in the slightest that the newfound object of your lust could possibly be a male, then he/she/it is. If you are still unsure, quietly ask one of the other girls in the bar or the *mamasan*. More often than not, they will tell you the truth because they know you will be really pissed of when you find out later that they lied. Sometimes it is almost impossible to tell so you should be absolutely certain before you do something you may regret.

This is one case when experience makes little difference. Many longtime Pattaya residents get caught even though they thought they could pick them out. One guy actually lived with a post-op katoey for three weeks and still could not tell that 'she' was once a 'he'.

CHAPTER

7

The *Fa-lung* on Holiday

*"Eagles may soar, but weasels don't
get sucked into jet engines"*

R ight from the beginning, I described Pattaya as being like Disneyland. Well, nothing has changed. Don't take any of the bar areas of Thailand too seriously because everything that happens here is just part of a game. Furthermore, it is *their* game, *their* pitch and *their* rules. Beating the Thai girls at their own game is next to impossible so don't waste your precious time and money trying.

You may be a big shot in your own country, making decisions every day that affect peoples lives but here you are a babe in the woods. The girls and some of Thailand's resident entrepreneurs have an arsenal of tricks and schemes that you would not believe.

> *The wiles and guiles that women work,*
> *Dissembled with an outward show,*
> *The tricks and toys that in them lurk,*
> *The cock that treads them shall not know.*
>   W. Shakespeare

(I just put that in to show you I done got me some book learnin'.)

The best you can hope for is to have a fantastic holiday while at the same time, limiting your losses. Liken it to a game of chess. Your delicate flower will perhaps use the *Noi Soisky Twosky* gambit, which involves money and a relative. *Your* money and one of *her* relatives. This can be countered by the tried and true *ATMsky Cardova Kaputsky* defense. Note that this defense can only be used once per game and is only good for twenty-four hours. However, if used on a Friday evening in conjunction with the *Banksky Closedikov* manoeuvre, it can be good for up to sixty-four hours. It's all a heap of fun.

Having spent many hours observing tourists coming and going, it appears that the *fa-lung* with the best win/loss statistics in the game are the ones who come here for no other reason than to enjoy themselves. Here for a good time, not a long time. They have a wife or girlfriend back home and have no intention of falling in love or attaching themselves to a Thai girl. They understand the precept that has been around since time began: Falling in love = heart swells + brain shrinks. When they leave, they go home with a smile and a fleeting memory of the face of the girl(s) who put it there. No names, just faces.

The worst at playing the Pattaya game are the guys who come here with more money than sense. They throw their money around like drunken sailors and overpay for every service at every opportunity. They think nothing of giving a girl from a Beer Bar 3,000 *baht* for a night or tipping with 100 *baht* notes everywhere they go. They think that, by doing so, they will be loved by all and sundry as well as buy the respect of the local people.

I've got news for these guys - and it's all bad. Firstly, you must have incredibly low self-esteem because you obviously believe the only way to get someone to like you is to throw money at them. Secondly, you are doing a disservice to your fellow *fa-lung* by giving Thais the impression that we are all rich and think nothing of paying exorbitant prices. Thirdly, you gain no respect from the local Thais because they realize you are just a big, stupid, walking ATM. Behind your back, they, especially the bar girls, laugh at your stupidity. Don't think I am joking, because I have sat and watched them do it.

The Butterfly

Welcome to the top of the Thai Bar Girl Shit List. It never ceases to amaze me how a guy who goes with two or five or ten different girls in a week is considered the lowest of the low - a 'butterfly', and yet a girl who goes with seven different *fa-lung* in as many nights is not. There appears to be bit of a double standard regarding the issue.

Comedian Woody Allen once quipped, "sex without love is a meaningless experience but, as meaningless experiences go, it's pretty damned good!" Basically, the idea of noncommittal sex with multiple partners is not a new one. It has been around since man first ventured out of his cave and clobbered the first female (not necessarily human) that he happened across. Once satisfied, he would return to his cave, fall asleep and wait until his primal urges rose again. To many of us, they were the good old days.

In the 21st Century, the caveman scenario is played out daily in the bar areas of Pattaya, Bangkok, Phuket and Chiang Mai. The modern day caveman, however, ventures out of his hotel and uses his wallet, not a club, to score the first female his loins desire. Once satisfied, he can bide his time until he again feels the need.

If you have come to Thailand to simply drown yourself in as many women and as much alcohol as your body can take, then all the advice under the sun is not going to save you. The short-time bars will be your happy hunting ground during the afternoons and early evenings. The Beer Bars and Go Go Bars can take care of your nights. If you are going to take girls back to your room for a sleepover, then you may find the following tip to be helpful.

TIP

Early in your stay (in fact, up until the last couple of nights) never go with a girl from a bar close to your hotel, especially if the bar has a clear view of the entrance. Start with the bars furthest away from your hotel and work your way back (so to speak). For example, if you are staying in

*South Pattaya, go to Naklua Road or Soi 2 on your first
night. If you are staying at Nana Hotel in Bangkok, venture
up to Soi Cowboy. There is no shortage of bars or girls to
choose from.*

The reason for this is simple. It is easier to get a girl than it is to
get rid of one. I have done my share of 'butterflying' and believe me,
the further the girl's apartment or bar is from your hotel, the better.

*I have had phone calls to my room at all hours of the
night. One girl even knocked on my door at 3:00am when
I already had another companion in the room. One had
her friends staking out my hotel, reporting my movements.
Yet another left me so many messages that I ended up
changing hotels just to get some peace. (These things
worried me for one other reason - it meant that I was
obviously being far too generous with the folding stuff.)*

I'm not saying that this type of thing will happen every time a
gentle and delicate Thai girl's heart is brutally crushed beneath your Doc
Martens, but it is very annoying when it does. Life was meant to be
easy.

TIP
*If possible, it is a good idea to change hotels at some
point of your stay. I have spoken to many fa-lung who do
this. It adds a bit of variety to your trip and reduces the
chances of you being annoyed by an ex-conquest. This
may be difficult during high season when most of the hotels
are fully booked.*

*PS. When you check out, don't tell the receptionist or the
doorman where you are going. Should a girl come looking
for you, they will blab.*

The Cheap Charlie

Coming in at fourth spot on the Bar Girl Shit List is the Cheap Charlie. To my fellow CC's out there, don't worry about it. Fourth spot is low on the list. Swindlers, cutthroats, rapists and other villains share third spot. Second spot is held by any *fa-lung* who leaves Thailand without taking down her bank account details.

Here for a week to ten days and have a limited budget? Do not despair. You can still have a great time - you just have to plan it better. Here is some advice on how to enjoy Pattaya on a shoestring.

1   Accommodation
    If you are a first-timer then you have probably pre-booked your accommodation so you are screwed. The best thing to do is take note of other places to stay next time. There will be a next time, trust me. This may take some legwork but it will be worth it to find good, cheap accommodation in an area that you like. As explained earlier, apartments can be good value. Rooms with air, at around 400 *baht* per day are plentiful.

2   Food
    For the CC who likes Thai food, it will fit well within budget. European food is relatively expensive. My advice, if you like *fa-lung* food occasionally, is to make it your breakfast. There are a few hotels that offer 'all you can eat' breakfasts for under 100 *baht*. The only problem with this is that they only offer it between say 7:00am and 1:00pm. After a few days (and nights) in Pattaya, you will realize that getting anywhere before 1:00pm is not as easy as it sounds.

    In the evening there are buffet dinners for under 200 *baht*. If you are looking for a free meal at night, take a walk around the bars until you find one having a party. These are easy to spot, as the bar will be covered with balloons and there will usually be a pig roasting over a portable spit out the front. The guys who do this regularly, members of the burgeoning expat community, are

111

branded 'balloon chasers' by the bar owners. So what! Every night, a bar somewhere will be having a birthday or anniversary party, put up balloons and provide free food for customers. Sit, buy a drink and eat.

3   Transport
In Pattaya, Baht Buses and motorcycle taxis are the only forms of public transport (excluding the 'free bus' which may no longer be in operation). Central Pattaya is so compact that, unless you have a medical condition or physical problem, walking is an alternative. At night, this may be inadvisable or impractical, especially when you have found a companion. In this case, if you are on Beach or Second Roads, tell her your large, white, air conditioned limousine will soon be along to pick you up. Then wait for the free bus (if it still exists).

4   Tipping
You do not have to tip in Thailand. I knew a group of three CCs who never left a tip at any bar, restaurant or hotel. These guys were well known by the locals as CCs but they were still liked, still got good service and still had a great time. Let's face it, if you go to a restaurant and four or five different bars each day and at each place leave a 20 *baht* tip, it soon adds up.

Having said that, I should point out that wages in Thailand for people in the service industry are very low so, if you did receive good service, it won't break you to leave a small tip in appreciation. Whatever you do, don't be a smart-arse and leave a 1 *baht* coin as a tip. Leaving 1 *baht* tip is a gross insult to Thais and will not be appreciated, even if you only did it in jest. It is better to leave no tip at all.

5   Drinks
Not an easy one for the CC. Drinks are the most expensive in the discos and nightclubs. At the Beer Bars the cheapest alcoholic drink will be the draught beer (if they have it) at around 50 *baht*. The price of bottled beer averages around 65 *baht*.

More and more bars are advertising 'Happy Hours' in an effort to attract customers and it is a good idea, while you are walking around, to check out these bars and times for future reference. I found one Beer Bar selling spirits for 15 *baht* per glass during happy hour and Go Go Bars have excellent value happy hours early in the evening. It is worth keeping your eyes open.

The cheapest drinks can be purchased from supermarkets and convenience stores but, all in all, even the true CC can not escape from paying for a few not-so-cheap drinks each day. The best advice is to drink slowly.

6   Girls

Just because you have a limited budget does not mean that you can not enjoy some feminine delights. The CC will not go with a girl from a Go Go Bar because the bar fines for these girls are too high, ranging from 500 to 1000 *baht* for the night, depending on the time of year. These girls also ask for much more money for personal services. The minimum is 1000 *baht* but I have heard some girls charge 3000 *baht*. Forget it.

Bar fines for the girls in the Beer Bars range from 200 *baht* to 300 *baht*. In Short-time Bars it will be 350 to 450 *baht* but that includes use of the room. An overnight guest from a Beer Bar will cost you between 500 and 1,000 *baht*. You may haggle any higher figure, but do it before you pay the bar fine.

In Soi 6 one afternoon, I asked a girl how much she wanted for a short time. She replied 800 baht. Knowing this figure to be outrageous, I told her 500 baht was the going rate. Her next offer was 700 but again I held my ground. Next, she asked for 500 plus a 100 baht 'tip'. Two minutes later, 500 baht was agreed upon.

The section on General Advice in Chapter 6 provides ways to save money once you have found yourself a more permanent companion.

CHAPTER

8

The *Fa-lung* in Love

"Sex is like air - it is not important unless you aren't getting any!"

There is a line from a song that goes, "looking for love in all the wrong places." If you are indeed looking for love, then Pattaya is the wrongest place on the planet.

To my knowledge, there is no bar girl walking around with "Pick me – I'm a good one!" tattooed on her forehead. Although most things are possible here, newcomers should never attempt to find the girl of their dreams until they have become very familiar with the place and Thai ways. It is difficult not to fall in love every day, but a little restraint in the beginning will prove invaluable later. Experienced *fa-lung* will tell you that the attrition rate when searching for the right girl, is astronomical. In layman's terms, this means that you are going to have to kiss a lot of frogs before you find your princess.

So many guys come here and fall in love with the first girl they meet. In some cases, he has spent so many years being rejected by women in his own country that he can not resist the first one who shows an interest in him, not helped by the fact she is probably beautiful and half his age.

In every case, he is misguided in the belief that she is the only one for him. In spite of warnings from well-meaning friends to take things slowly and play the field until he learns more about the place, he is convinced she is 'different' and he can't live without her.

Perhaps the problem lies with Western moralists who for centuries have been preaching that 'love' and 'sex' are equated. We have been told that sex is an act of love and should come as a result of the love. 'Love' is an integral part of, and should always precede, 'sex'. The difference here is that, for Thais, sex is simply another bodily function which is separate to and can precede 'love'.

For many Western men, a Thai bar girl indicating a 'desire' to sleep with him and the subsequent act itself sends him a message that she loves him. He overlooks the fact that a financial transaction also took place, justifying it by saying the money was his 'gift' to her rather than her 'fee'. He blindly forgets that having sex for money is her 'job' and is totally different to having sex with someone she loves.

The tragedy of this scenario is that a supposedly intelligent man, after half a century of bad luck or bad judgement, can travel half way around the world and, within the space of five minutes, believe he has the greatest stroke of luck by finding the only bar girl who is 'different'.

TIP

Always fall in love with a girl named 'Lek'. It saves a lot of confusion later.
Girlfriend Selection Criteria:

Hair:	*Black*
Complexion:	*Dark*
Eyes:	*Brown*
Name:	*Lek*

That limits the field down to about 10,000.

Seriously though, before you find yourself falling hopelessly in love with a Thai girl, there are some important things that you should know.

Girls to Avoid

If you are simply looking for short-times and brief flings, the field is open and the choice of partner is completely up to you. If you are thinking about a more substantial relationship, then there are some easily recognizable warning signs to look out for. Statistically, the following bar girl types have a poor track record when it comes to maintaining serious relationships:

1   Those wearing an abundance of gold chains, bracelets etc.
    Basically, a girl can not afford to buy a lot of gold jewellery unless she has a *fa-lung* sponsor or many *fa-lung* boyfriends. These girls are very 'street-wise', demand more money for their time and know exactly how to extract every extra $ from men. Unless your name is Bill Gates and you whisk her away to live happily ever after, she is not likely to give up her other 'friends' for you.

2   Those carrying mobile phones.
    In the original *Money Number One* I wrote, "No bar girl can afford to maintain a mobile phone unless she has a regular boyfriend paying the bills. In fact, these girls probably have many boyfriends and I'll bet each one gets the phone bill."

    Things have changed over the past four years and the bar girls of Pattaya have embraced the cellular communication revolution with unbridled enthusiasm. It is now almost impossible to find a bar girl who does not have a mobile phone. The prices have dropped sufficiently so even the new arrivals can afford one. Still, be aware that it is an asset to her, not an asset to you.

    I witnessed a Thai girl talking to her fa-lung lover on her mobile. She spoke good English. Her current boyfriend sitting beside her was German and did not understand much English. Otherwise, he would have heard her tell the (absent) love-of-her-life how much she missed him and how she was waiting for him to come back to her.

"No darling, I not go with other *fa-lung*.
Only wait for you."

117

It is impossible to keep track of any girl by calling her mobile number. She could be anywhere and with anybody as the previous story illustrates. At least if she only has the phone in her room, you know exactly where she is each time you phone her.

3   Those who tell you that they live alone.
Apart from the obvious financial obstacles to living alone, there are some other things you should understand. Any girl who tells you that she lives alone is probably lying.

My first girlfriend (I've mentioned her before) told me that she lived in an apartment alone. Every afternoon she would return to her room to change clothes, do the washing etc, then meet me back at my hotel at 8.00pm. After a month or so, I told her "I'll come with you. I want to see your apartment." Well, it was like I had just run over her grandmother and raped her cat. "You can not come my apartment. I never take fa-lung to my apartment." With that, she walked out.

Next day she turned up at my hotel, apologized in her Thai way and said that if I still wanted to see her apartment, I could. It did not take an Einstein to work out that whatever it was that she did not want me to see had now been removed and her room had been made 'safe' for me to look over. I went anyway.

To cut a long story short, I was always suspicious after that. I would turn up at her apartment without warning. One day I noticed that she was in a particular hurry to get me to leave. She had just had a shower, was dressing very quickly and the bathroom door was closed. Before she ushered me out of her room, I made an excuse to use the bathroom. In spite of her protestations, I opened the door. Guess what I found? There was a stark naked Thai man hiding behind the door. It turned out that he was her boyfriend/pimp who she had been living with for three years. He was a motorcycle taxi driver who would also send her 'customers' from time to time. I was paying the rent for that bastard!

My story is not unique, but I hope you get the point without me having to relate any more sad tales. Not many girls truly live alone.

TIP

If you are really keen on a girl who says that she lives by herself, then check out her apartment. Don't give her advance warning. If she makes any excuse whatsoever as to why you can not come with her, get rid of her. Do not let her make any phone calls or talk to any of her friends on the way and be very suspicious of any delaying tactics. Unless you have her enthusiastic agreement, she has something to hide.

4   Those who have been working in a bar for more than three months. I used to think six months was the cutoff figure but it seems they are getting smarter.

These girls should be avoided because, if she has been working for any length of time, she becomes conditioned. She has learned every trick in the book and knows exactly how to extract every $ from you. 'Money Number One' has been burned into her brain. Remember, any girl who comes to work bar is not from the social elite of Thailand. She is a simple girl from Wherethefuckaburi who has no job at home and so comes to earn money to support herself, her child and her family. Her formal education will be limited or nonexistent.

On arrival, 90% of the girls can not speak a word of English. They are, however, very intelligent and quick learners. Those who have been working bars for more than three months are easy to spot because they will know how to speak English. As well as having learned English, they will have learned the tricks of the trade from the other girls. She may have also established a number of regular boyfriends.

My advice is to avoid these girls if your intention is to find a long-term girlfriend. "What is the point of getting a girlfriend that can not speak English?" I hear you ask. The answer is that it is a trade-off, a compromise. Believe me, there are other ways to communicate besides talking. Once you have won her heart, you can teach her to speak English while, at the same time, you should learn to speak Thai.

5 Those who appear to have an older 'brother' hanging around or somewhere in the picture.
Why? Because the guy is probably not her brother. Most often he is her boyfriend or husband. I could be wrong, but I doubt it. Don't bother trying to check it out by asking her friends because they will not tell you the truth.

6 Those who sport a tattoo with the words "I love John" and your name is Fred.
Any person - male, female, Thai or *fa-lung* - who would have the name of someone else tattooed on their body has sawdust for brains.

The girl sitting behind the bar had the words, "Property of Johnny" tattooed in a circle on her shoulder. I asked her if she knew what it meant. No idea. I then asked where Johnny was. She said they were finished. I'm sure, at the time, Johnny thought it was a great joke but now that poor girl has to wear her offensive graffiti forever.

Financial Support

There is no such thing as a free lunch and this is particularly true in the bars. Any *fa-lung* who has had a long-term relationship with a Thai bar girl will confirm that it is a more expensive exercise than remaining a single, devil-may-care butterfly. (In fact this not only applies to Thai bar girls but, as married men throughout the world will tell you, also seems to apply to women everywhere. But I digress.)

The first thing *fa-lung* do once they think they have found the girl of their dreams is tell her to stop working bar. It is in our nature to do so. We all want our girlfriend to be kind, loving, honest and faithful. Well gentlemen, I have some good news and some bad news. The good news is that the 'kind' and 'loving' requirements can be met, in most cases, with a little patience. The bad news is that the 'honest' and 'faithful' criteria will require a more substantial effort from both of you.

The moment you ask your lady love to stop working bar, she will agree. In her very next breath she will say something like "You give me money for food, for room, for Mama." This is a reasonable request. To her, the money is to compensate for the lack of income she would get from the bar work. To you, the money is to buy her loyalty and faithfulness. One of you is sadly mistaken. Guess which one?

For expedience, I will limit this discussion to Pattaya but you could substitute Bangkok, Phuket or Chiang Mai. Her idea is that she remains in Pattaya, waiting for your return. You go back to work and, every month, send money to support her. On page 123 is a fictitious letter comprising various reasons given by the bar girls to their *fa-lung* boyfriends as to why he should send them (more) money. Each reason has been used many times and the list is by no means complete. Once you give a bar girl your postal address or e-mail address, expect to receive a letter or e-mail, not exactly the same as the example but with similar intention.

Apart from extraordinary expenses (sick buffalo etc), her monthly cost of living is around 3,000 *baht* if she shares a room with other girls.

121

However, the standard amount that she will ask for is 10,000 *baht* per month. This seems to be the accepted first offer but is by no means the bottom line. I know some guys who send only 5,000 *baht* but I suspect that this may not be enough to ensure her faithfulness. Don't forget, she will also be sending money home to her family.

Before you tell her to stop work, agree to send her money or do anything else, please think about it very seriously. If she remains in Pattaya, there is no way that she can or will remain honest and faithful to you. There are just too many other *fa-lung* here presenting too many temptations for her to make some extra cash. Her friends will also put pressure on her. For bar girls, it is not the quality, generosity or kindness of her one *fa-lung* boyfriend that measures her prestige among the other girls but the quantity of generous *fa-lung* boyfriends she can accumulate.

There are three options, my friend, as to how you handle it. Firstly, you can choose to live in a fool's paradise by accepting her at her word and looking the other way when suspicion or jealousy raise their ugly heads. Secondly, you can continually beat your head against a brick wall, stress yourself out to the point of a stroke and maintain a continuous guard on her in an attempt to keep her on the straight and narrow.

> *I was introduced to a girl who, I was told later, used to work bar but quit because she had three fa-lung boyfriends, each from a different country. Two of them send her 10,000 baht per month and the other sends her 20,000 baht a month. This girl does not work any more because takes home 40,000 baht (US$1,000) each month. She does not need to work. I asked what happens when two or all of her boyfriends turn up in Pattaya at the same time. The reply was a shrug of the shoulders. Since then, I have been told of at least two other girls who receive in excess of 100,000 baht a month in exactly the same fashion.*

The third option is to tell her that you will only support her if she leaves Pattaya. She can either go back to stay at her home in the country or move to a place of your choosing. If she refuses to leave, then I'm

Dear (fa-lung)* insert your name here
I love you and miss you too much. Now I have problem.
I tell you before that buffalo me sick. Now it die. Fall
down dead in middle of rice field. Unfortunately, when it
fall, it land on Papa and break his leg in three places.
Now he can not work. Brother me make stretcher from
bamboo she take from roof of house. Then roof collapse
and rain get in house. She take Papa to hospital on
motorcycle. She have accident coming home. Run into
police car. Brother me to blame. Police say he have to
pay big money. Motorcycle OK. Police car kaput. Now
give Mama have heart problem. Doctor say she need
triple bypass. I not understand what is. He say you
understand. Up to now I only work cashier in bar and
not go with man. I wait for you come back Pattaya. If
you will not help me I have to go with many many many
many more fa-lung to pay bills. The old people in my
village in Wherethefuckaburi think that it is all your
fault. If you had send me money to buy medicine for sick
buffalo when I ask you, then it not die, Papa not break
leg, house still have roof, brother not ride into Police car
and Mama not have heart problem. Please send for me
200,000 baht for my bank account. Papa fix: 10,000
New roof: 30,000 New Police car: 100,000 Mama fix:
50,000. I take off 2,000 baht for sell buffalo meat but
have to pay more hospital bill for 24 people have
problem eat contaminated meat - 12,000 baht. I not
know money Australia but my friend me say it about
26.598755 baht approximately. This mean you send me
10,000 dollar Australia. Little bit money for you. I love
you too much.
Lek

afraid she is just another gold-digger and my advice would be to not waste your money on her. If she agrees, you can feel more comfortable – not secure, just comfortable. You should then ensure that she moves all her belongings while you are there to supervise. Do not accept her 'promise' to undertake the move while you are back home sorting out your affairs. She is certain to come up with some excuse as to why she can not move house this month. Send more money.

If all goes well and she does leave Pattaya, then you can pat yourself on the back. She really does like you. You have become a member of a very small club of foreigners who have won the heart of a Thai girl. Now, you have to make good all of your promises to her. Her cost of living at her home in the countryside will be no less than that of Pattaya. Probably higher, because here she will be regarded as a source of cash by all her friends, relatives and neighbours.

Don't let her get bored. Country life can be pretty mundane for a girl who has lived the excitement of the bar scene, so you have to keep her occupied. This may involve paying for her to attend a course or setting up a small business for her to be involved in. Don't expect the business to make any money for you (Read Chapter 11), so don't go overboard. It is only to keep her occupied.

At this point there are so many things that could happen and so many variables that it is impossible to guide you further. You will have to play it by ear. Three things you should do if you reach this stage are:

1   If her home does not have a telephone, pay for one to be installed. <u>Do not</u> buy her a mobile phone – EVER!

2   Visit her or bring her to visit you as often as possible. Don't just come to Thailand once a year for your annual three or four week vacation and expect her to fall all over you. That old expression, "absence makes the heart grow fonder" is a total load of crap.

3   When you visit her, it is a good idea not to tell her when you are arriving. It is amazing the amount of information you can get when you turn up unexpectedly. It is an excellent way of testing her honesty and loyalty. At least it will keep her on her toes.

Going on 'Holiday'

So far, I have spent a lot of ink trying to convince you just how much Thais love Thailand. This is not to say that they don't mind getting out of the place from time to time, especially if someone else is paying. Good girls go to heaven, Pattaya girls go everywhere.

Getting the object of your lust to agree to go on holiday with you is not a problem. Just ask. I give you a 100% guarantee that her answer will be an emphatic "Yes!" If you have been going with her for a long time (more than three consecutive nights), she may not even wait for you to ask.

Taking her with you for trips within Thailand initially is probably a good idea. She can be your interpreter while you assess how good a 'traveller' she is. Other countries present a different challenge. Almost half of the bar girls I have asked already have their passports. If not, getting a passport for her is neither difficult nor expensive. It merely involves two trips to Bang Na in Bangkok and about 1,050 *baht*.

You may experience problems with visas depending on which country you wish to take her to. Travel to another ASEAN country is the easiest because Thais usually (CHECK FIRST!) can obtain a 'visa on entry'. I have taken girls to Hong Kong and the Philippines without any problem.

If you have decided to take her home to meet mother, then organize it so that you accompany her. Do not just leave her with a refundable air ticket or the money to buy a ticket and then tell her that you will meet her at some foreign airport. The reasons for this are threefold:

(a)   If you leave her a refundable ticket or the money for a ticket, you can be certain that before it comes time for her to fly off into your arms, she will have found better uses for the money. You will be told of some 'emergency' or family crisis that required the immediate influx of (your) funds in order to solve. Send more money.

(b)   She is Thai. Her English is limited and even though she has a
        passport, she will have to fill out the immigration and customs
        form on the plane. Even if she can speak English, her written
        English skills will be nonexistent. The Immigration Form has a
        space for 'Home Address'. The very second she writes 'Pattaya'
        in that space, Immigration Officers all over the world hear alarm
        bells. The problem does not end there. What does she write in
        the space marked 'Occupation'?

(c)   She is Thai. She loves Thai food. The thought of not eating
        Thai food for seven or more days is simply too torturous for her
        to contemplate. She will therefore decide to bring some of her
        favourite food and essential ingredients with her. You can tell
        her not to until you are blue in the face but it is no use. As well
        as a problem with Immigration, she now has a problem with
        Customs. The sniffer-dogs at the airport will do backflips when
        they get a whiff of your lady-love's suitcase.

She can return home to Thailand by herself without a problem,
but definitely travel with her on the forward trip. On the Immigration
form, she can put her actual home address in the province. Not Pattaya.
As for 'Occupation', I would never tell you to lie to the lovely Immigration
people (in case one is reading this now), but I would suggest that she not
write 'bar girl'.

As for the food dilemma, you should supervise the packing of
her suitcase. That way you can throw out any items that may cause the
ire of Customs Officers.

Understand also that most Thais do not like cold weather. To
them 'cold' is anything under 28°C. If you are considering taking her
to England or Europe in winter, then prepare yourself for constant
complaining. One week of cold weather and she will want to go home.
One week of her constant moaning and you will be happy to send her
home.

Correspondence

Marriage guidance counsellors preach that communication is the most important part of any successful relationship. It has been my experience that it is difficult enough for a man to communicate with a woman of his own nationality. Women seem to speak a different language to men. Women understand the words alright, but string a few together into a coherent sentence and they put a whole new meaning to it. For instance, a man telling his wife, "Sorry I'm late darling, but there was a terrible accident on the freeway and we were held up for two hours. I tried to call you but the battery in my mobile was dead", is interpreted as, "I stayed out to have a few beers with my mates because I don't love you and don't care how long it took you to prepare dinner." Communicating with your Thai girlfriend is even trickier.

I flew back to Australia for what was supposed to be a six month working stint. My girlfriend, Lek, had come to Don Muang airport to see me off before heading home to Korat (where else?) to take care of mama and papa while I was away. Before boarding, I took a photo of the plane to finish off my roll of film. After about a week in Australia, I wrote a letter to Lek enclosing some of the photos I had taken. On the back of the photograph of the plane, I wrote 'My plane' in Thai.

A couple of weeks later I received an e-mail from Lek. It was in English and contained the usual 'love you' and 'miss you' stuff. What really made me laugh was her comment on the photo.
"It is not really your plane, is it? It is the plane of Thai Airways International. You don't have to lie to me, darling." I laughed even louder when I thought about what a commotion the photo must have caused at chez Lek.
"Does he really own a plane?"
"Is he very rich?"
"No, he is a lying bastard. That is a Thai Airways plane."

It proved just how difficult it is to translate exact English meaning into Thai. An English person, reading 'my plane' on the back of the photograph would immediately realize that I meant 'this is the plane that I flew on'. When I translated 'my plane' into Thai, it came across as 'the plane that belongs to me'.

Every relationship endures periods of separation. Whether it be for one week or six months, maintaining the relationship for the time the two of you are apart requires frequent communication. The telephone is obviously the best method of keeping in contact but international calls are expensive. Writing a letter is cheap but takes too long to arrive. Some letters never arrive at all. More and more bar girls rely on e-mail to keep track of their overseas boyfriends. E-mail is relatively cheap and instantaneous. However, it still has its problems.

She won't write to you in Thai as she knows that you will probably not be able to find a Thai translator in your own country. She will draft the letter in Thai and pay for it to be translated into English. She may take the letter to a translation service where, for a fee (around 30 *baht* per page), they will translate it for her. Many Internet Cafes will translate and type the e-mail for her as part of their service. It does not matter if the girl is not computer literate.

Sounds simple doesn't it? The problem arises because most of the translators are Thai nationals who have learned English. They have learned very simple English and they make mistakes. They not only make mistakes translating her Thai into English, but also in translating your e-mail into Thai.

Using the K.I.S.S. Principle, here are some suggestions for writing to your girlfriend:

1   No colloquialisms.
    The Thai manager of the hotel was in a highly confused
    state. He had just received an e-mail from a guy who
    wished to change the dates of his booking. The e-mail
    began, "Sorry to be such a bloody pest...". The manager

had no idea what the writer meant by that. His first thought was the guy was complaining that the hotel was full of vermin bleeding all over the place.

2   No slang.
"This bloke is a good mate."
Most Australians and many English people will understand exactly what is meant by that statement. In most other parts of the world, it may confuse the reader. The word 'bloke' may not appear in smaller dictionaries and 'mate' may not have its slang meaning mentioned. The statement will probably make no sense to Thais at all.

3   Short sentences with only one verb in each.
I am ashamed to admit that I once wrote to a bar girl that she was "so beautiful I don't believe you would not have many boyfriends." Sickening stuff, I know. Her friend called me from Pattaya and told me that my girlfriend was very upset when she got my letter and had cried uncontrollably. I could not understand why until I got back and read the translation provided for her. It read "You are beautiful. I don't believe you. You have many boyfriends." It took a lot of slow talking to assure her that was not what I meant.

4   Short, simple common words.
"I am continually overwhelmed by joyous anticipation of our impending reunion" may make sense to your English professor but will only confuse a Thai girl. Try "I can not wait to see you again" or "I miss you" instead.

Once you have finished drafting your letter, read it back. If it sounds rather childish, then you have succeeded. Those are the easiest letters to translate and there is a good chance the meaning will not be lost.

The In-Laws

*"The perfect Thai girlfriend - an orphan
with no friends or living relatives!"*

This is one of the standard jokes among foreign Pattayaholics. She is what we are all looking for but, to my knowledge, nobody has found yet. If they have, they have kept very quiet about it. The reason for the needle-in-a-haystack search will become obvious to you once you have established a long-term relationship (more than three consecutive nights) with your dream girl.

Visiting the Relatives

At some point, you may be invited to visit her family back in the province. The only way you will not be invited is if she does not really like you or she has taken too many *fa-lung* home already.

A Thai girl is socially restricted in the number of different *fa-lung* she can take home to meet the family. She may get away with two but never more than three. This is because, when her *fa-lung* arrives at her village, he is the talking point of the whole place. Everyone, and I mean everyone, will come out to see the *fa-lung* that *Noi*, *Nok* or *Lek* has brought home. She may be able to explain (lie) why this *fa-lung* is not the same as the last one she brought home but, after the third one, she will probably lose face and be known as what we in the West refer to as a 'cheap girl'. This is social suicide for both her and her family.

The lesson from this, as far as you are concerned, is that if you are not invited to visit, it is best not to continue seriously. It will mean that she either does not really like you or she has exceeded the maximum number of boyfriends socially acceptable to bring home. In either case it is probably better for you to look elsewhere.

If you have been invited to go to her home, be warned that it can be very EXPENSIVE. By all means, go. It is a great experience and a good break from the rigours of bar life but be prepared both emotionally and financially. Your hand and your wallet will begin a new, committed and continuous relationship. They will not be separated for more than five minutes.

There are three ways you can get to her home. By bus/train, hire car with driver or hire a car and drive yourself. The bus or train is by far the cheapest method but it is long, arduous and not very convenient as it sometimes leaves or arrives at odd hours. Your lady will know all about the bus because this is her means of transport each time she returns home for a visit. Hiring a car or minibus with a driver is easy, much more convenient and comfortable, but obviously more expensive. If you have the confidence (and watertight comprehensive Insurance) to hire a car and drive yourself, remember that even though the roads in Thailand are excellent, the drivers are not. This last method is much more socially acceptable than arriving at Mama's house by bus and your lady will be delighted to roll up to her home in a nice shiny car.

TIP
Do not get sucked into taking any of her friends with you. On my first trip up country, my lady asked if she could bring her friend along. Being a kind and generous (and stupid) fa-lung, I agreed. The Thai language does not have plurals, so when she said "friend" she really meant

131

"friends". I ended up with five girls squeezed into my car. Guess who pays? The second time, I put my foot down and said only one friend was allowed. This turned out to be almost as bad since the two of them yakked to each other the entire trip and totally ignored me. They then argued over directions and led me out of the way. In short, only take your girlfriend with you - nobody else.

TIP
Buy mosquito repellent before you leave.

TIP
If you elect to drive yourself, obtain a road map before you leave and determine the best route. Your girlfriend will probably only know the way the bus goes. Unfortunately, as we know, the bus does not necessarily take the most direct route. It may go through every population centre, every one-horse town and every back street to get there. Unless you want to waste time (but see a lot of the countryside), work out the best route before leaving Pattaya. When you get near her village or town, your girlfriend can take over with directions to her home.

The negative reassessment of your disposable cash begins before you leave. Your little darling can not possibly return to her home with the same rags and borrowed clothing that she has been wearing around town. A new wardrobe is called for so that Mama will be impressed by her daughter's rise up the social ladder on the back of your Visa card. Her village must also see physical evidence that she has found a kind and generous *fa-lung*. You will therefore also be required to bring 'gifts' for her friends and family. This usually means clothing and food.

Being a fair-minded sort of chap, I thought, "OK. I will be eating at their home, so bringing some rice, chili and other foodstuffs is the least I can do." Wrong! My girlfriend did the shopping and we arrived with a 40kg sack of rice, the largest bag of dried chili I have ever seen, half a pig and enough green vegetables to feed the entire population of a small country. Oh, and yes, beer - two dozen large bottles.

On arrival at the home, be prepared that the house may be primitive by Western standards. It will, however, be clean and tidy. Remove your shoes before entering any Thai house. Next comes another interesting Thai custom. In Western societies, when a guest is taken to meet the family, he is usually introduced to everyone present. Not so in Thailand. You will be very lucky if you are even introduced to Mama and Papa. By this time you should know how to say "*sa-wut dee krup*" and to '*wai*'. Once you have done this you will be virtually ignored. If her father actually says "*sa-wut dee krup*" to you, it will be the only time you will get any recognition from him. Most likely, he will then disappear. You will be offered a seat and then your girlfriend and her family will catch up on all the gossip - for hours. To be fair, the family is probably very shy with strangers and nobody, apart from your girlfriend and maybe some of the schoolchildren, will speak a word of English. Do not expect your girlfriend to do any translating for you either. She will probably ignore you too. In the West, we would consider this behaviour very rude. Here in Thailand, it is normal.

You will be offered food. It would be bad manners to refuse. Saying that you are not hungry (even if it is true) won't cut it either. Try everything offered to you, even if it is only one mouthful and learn to say "*a-loi*" (delicious). However, do not drink the water. This is where the beer you should have purchased earlier comes in handy.

I'm sure there are a couple of Thai families around that are convinced I'm an alcoholic because I only drank beer, even for breakfast. I did avoid illness though.

Once the sun starts to go down, it is time to reach for the mosquito repellent. Thai mosquitoes are ferocious, clever and hungry for *fa-lung* blood. Drown your body in repellent. Mosquito coils have limited success and mosquito nets represent only a minor obstacle to the bloodthirsty little devils.

During your visit you may have to refrain from cuddling and kissing your girlfriend in front of other people. Traditional Thais (not so much those in Pattaya or Bangkok) frown on public displays of affection between people of the opposite sex. If you wish to know more about this, there are many books on the subject of Thai etiquette. Let your girlfriend take the lead. She will not do anything to offend her family so follow her direction.

She will probably take you to meet everyone she knows, or should I say, she will take you to show you off to everyone she knows. Just as the Romans would bring their captives home to Rome and parade them through the streets for all to see, you will be her trophy. And you won't go alone. If you have a hired car, it will always be packed to capacity with her friends and relatives who will all come out of the woodwork with an abundance of imaginative financial woes. Be prepared. Wherever you go, whatever you do, you will be paying for everything and everybody. I'm afraid there is no way out of it.

Some guys have told me they were treated like kings and not allowed to pay for anything during their visit to her home. This does happen but the family was probably more affluent than most. Their time will come.

Before leaving the nest there is one final duty to perform. You will be required to leave a gift for Mama. This time it is money. If you ask your girlfriend "How much should I give?", she will invariably say "Up to you". This is a trick answer. If you leave too little, your girlfriend will lose face in front of her family. If you leave too much, it becomes a precedent and leaving anything less the next time you visit will be greeted less favourably. The only guide I can give you is to say that 1,000 *baht* is not going to be enough. Don't worry too much, because your girlfriend will respond to your laughably inadequate initial offer by amending it upward to a more respectable figure anyway.

All in all though, your trip upcountry will be enjoyable and necessary if you plan to stay with your girlfriend long-term. You will be treated well and get to see some of the 'real' Thailand.

When the Relatives Visit You

If Mohammed doesn't go to the mountain then sooner or later, the mountain will come to Mohammed. This mountain comes in the form of her freeloading relatives. Once you have set up a little love nest for yourself and the apple of your loins, you may be asked if one or more of her relatives can come for a visit. Then again, you may not even be asked. Usually it will be her child or children she wishes to bring, closely followed by Mama, Papa, sisters, brothers, 22nd cousins etc.

Her request will be sweetened by lots of extra TLC to help you make up your mind in her favour. You're a kind-hearted guy and, what the hell, it's only for a couple of days, right? Well my friend, it is time to bite the bullet. It is time to be hard and tough. Say an emphatic "No!". No matter how bad this may make you feel or no matter what argument ensues with your loved-one, you are far better off than enduring the horrors that can be wrought by your newly-acquired in-laws. They have been known to cause a bigger rift in a perfectly happy relationship than an Exocet missile. To be fair, consider the pros and cons:

The Cons

1 You really don't know how many relatives are going to show up at your door. You may be told that only one parasite is coming to visit, then two or three will come knocking. "Sister me come visit" may mean her sister, sister's husband and five ankle-biters. As a rule of thumb, the number of visitors quoted by your girlfriend is the minimum number. The maximum is the population of her village.

2 You will be expected to pay for everything, and I mean everything. If you get off without paying for their bus fare, you are doing well, but don't pat yourself on the back yet. You will probably be asked to reimburse the cost later. You will pay for all food, all gifts, all transport and even the three *baht* if they happen to want to go to the toilet on one of the many all-expenses-paid nights on the town. Lastly, you will fork out for their trip home. By that time, you will gladly pay it.

135

" *Tee-ruk*! Mama's here!"

The love of my life went home for a couple of days and returned with her daughter and sister. I was told only the daughter was coming. On the second day, while out sightseeing, daughter spots a large stuffed doll on a hawker's van. She likes. She wants. My negative response was greeted with daggers from my hitherto affectionate girlfriend. "Why you not buy for she? She like. You no love she? You no love me?" Total fury.

"No, I'm not going to buy the ungrateful little brat an overpriced toy that I will get no thanks for and she'll destroy in five minutes."

This, naturally, when translated into Thai, came out as "Of course, my darling, how stupid of me. I love your daughter as if she were my own and her wish is my command." Daughter happy. Girlfriend happy. Don't mention it.

3   You will receive little or no outward signs of affection from your sweetheart for the duration of the stay. As for sex, it is out of the question. You will be lucky if you retain your bed. If Mama comes, you won't. It'll be the floor for you.

4   Your property will be treated as their property. Before they arrived, what was yours was hers. Now that they are here, what is yours is theirs. Mama will do a mental calculation of the value of all your assets. If she finds something she likes, your girlfriend will be told to bring it with her the next time she goes home. All your shampoo, toothpaste and other toiletries will be used up like there is no tomorrow and if they happen to break something of yours, it will be laughed off. "You *fa-lung*. You can buy one more." Count the silverware before they leave.

5   You will receive no thanks for whatever you do.

The Pros
There are none.

CHAPTER

10

The *Fa-lung* inSane

"A successful man is one who makes more money than his wife can spend. A successful woman is one who can find such a man."

You don't have to be in the final stages of brain deterioration due to thirty or forty years of alcohol abuse to consider marriage to a Thai bar girl, but it helps. It would also help if you could read (Thai) minds, because the chasm between her intention and your comprehension would make the Grand Canyon look like a bee's navel.

On a more positive note, there are very few girls in Thailand just sitting around waiting to marry a foreigner, so don't think that you can simply fly into the country, flash your pearly-whites and run to the altar. Remember, her first priority is to provide financially for herself and her family. If she believes this can be achieved by marrying you, then she may consider it but, in truth, she would rather marry a Thai man.

This is in spite of what the girls may tell you about not liking Thai men. Among those I have spoken to (not only bar girls), Thai men, in general, have a poor reputation when it comes to making ideal partners. So why would a Thai girl prefer to marry someone like this instead of a kind and generous foreigner like you? I read somewhere that the girls, and probably Thais in general, like consistency. They know that a Thai husband may consistently get drunk, consistently cheat on them and consistently resort to violence in marital disputes. Mothers teach their daughters how to address these problems or, at least, how to cope with them. (I suspect that it may also have something to do with the Thai man speaking the same language and having the same culture and interests.)

Foreign men, on the other hand, are a complete mystery to the average Thai girl. Apart from the obvious language and cultural differences, she has no idea what to expect from a *fa-lung* husband. This is enough to scare the living hell out of her and propel her to a life that, as bad as it may be, at least she can understand.

In the majority of cases, Thai bar girls appear so gentle, accommodating, loving, caring, doting, subservient and so willing to please that you could be excused for thinking you have died and gone to heaven.

> *At meals, my Thai girlfriend would painstakingly remove all the bones from my fish, even the small ones, before serving it to me. She would also taste the food to make sure it was OK for me. My fa-lung ex-wife, on the other hand, used to just throw me a dead fish and squawk "Cook it yourself!"*

However, before you do anything stupid, re-read the list of the Thai bar girl's order of importance in Chapter 5. Have it tattooed on a prominent part of your anatomy, because your position on this list WILL NEVER CHANGE. You are at Number 13 now and no wedding ring, certificate or ceremony will move you up a single notch.

To those foreign men considering taking the plunge, please take some time to talk to some expats in Thailand. The horror stories related by *fa-lung* who have previously attempted this insanity would fill enough volumes to make Encyclopedia Britannica look like a post card. The true success stories could be carved on the back of a postage stamp with an axe.

MONEY *Still* NUMBER ONE

A An Englishman, close to retirement age, fell in love in Pattaya. He and his girlfriend decided to get married when he retired, at which time he would come to live with her in Thailand. For five years he spent every holiday with her and, when back at work, he sent money to support her. He saved and planned everything, including liquidating all his assets just before he finished up work so that he could settle down in Thailand with the love of his life. A few days before he caught the plane to Bangkok for the last time, he inexplicably transferred all his money into his intended's bank account in Thailand. When he arrived, guess what? Her bank account was empty and his money and his future wife were gone - never to be seen again.

B A fa-lung fell in love with the most beautiful Thai girl you could ever hope to see. For years he provided her with everything she wanted - money, car, house - and even started a business for her to manage. One day, with no prior warning and no reason forthcoming, she announced that she was getting back together with her fa-lung ex-boyfriend.

C An Englishman married a bar girl from Pattaya. They moved to the UK and lived together for five years. Each year they made several trips back to Thailand for holidays and all appeared rosy. One day, after receiving a phone call from Thailand, the lady told him that she had to go home. He replied that his work commitments were such that, if she waited a couple of weeks, they could go together and have a holiday. She then dropped the bombshell by telling him that she had to leave immediately because her 'husband' had called to tell her she could come home now. It turned out that she was already married to a Thai man when she married him. The money he had been sending home to her family actually went to her 'real' husband to enable him to build a house and set up a *business. When the house was finished, he called to tell her to come home. Her job was done.*

D   *With the wedding planned for next year, the fa-lung bought a house for himself and his Thai fiancee. Since foreigners can not own land in Thailand, he bought it in his lady's name, filled it with furniture and all was well. On his return from a seven-day business trip, he was surprised to find that his key did not fit the lock on the front door. He knocked on the door and was even more surprised when a stranger answered the door. "Who are you and what are you doing in my house?" he asked.*
"Your house?" came the reply. "This is my house. I only just bought it!"
Further investigation revealed that, while he was away, the little woman had been very busy indeed. She sold the house, all his furniture and was never seen again.

E   *An American fell in love in Pattaya. He was not a poor man, and he and his girlfriend decided to marry. When he was in Pattaya, she stayed with him at his hotel. When he was away, he sent money to support her. One day he arranged to meet her at a restaurant. When she did not show up at the appointed time, he decided to go back to his hotel. Opening the door to his room, he was shocked to find his fiancee in bed with another fa-lung. Apparently, she had met this other guy at a bar and went 'short-time' with him for 500 baht. She even used her fiancee's hotel room. The American threw them both out.*

I have told this last story to many Thais. In every case, their reaction was the same – nothing. A *fa-lung*, on hearing this story, would shake his head in disbelief at the girl's lack of forethought, throwing away what may have been a bright future for a lousy 500 *baht*. Thais stand there with blank looks on their faces as if to say, "So? What is the point of your story?" To them, the girl's behaviour was perfectly understandable.

MONEY *Still* NUMBER ONE

If you are intent on marrying a Thai girl, then for your own sake, follow these six pieces of advice:

1   You control the money. Never divulge exactly how much money you have in your bank. Do not open a joint bank account. Do not tell her the PIN number of your ATM card. Give her an allowance and a budget and insist that she stick to it.
2   Learn to speak Thai. It may be necessary to pay for Thai lessons because it is extremely difficult to pronounce the words correctly unless you actually listen to a Thai person saying them. The Thai phrasebooks are fine if you merely wish to know a few words and phrases, but finding a book that really teaches the language and more importantly, the grammar, is more difficult.

I have a Thai/English English/Thai dictionary. The only problem is that it has left out a lot of Thai words and expressions I hear every day and included many English words that are never used. When was the last time you used the word 'scurvy' in a sentence? How about 'bloodbath', 'dextral' or 'putsch'? I don't even know what those last two mean in English. I do however, now know how to say them in Thai if the occasion should ever arise.

3   Seek competent legal advice before putting any property into your future wife's name. There are legal ways to protect yourself and your property.
4   Once you are married, if you wish to reside in Thailand, do not live in Pattaya and settle as far away from her relatives and friends as possible. Find a nice place where she knows no-one. If you don't, the very second it becomes known that *Lek* has married a *fa-lung*, every one of her relatives, as well as every person she has ever said "hello" to in her life will come out of the woodwork to grab some of the action. The pressure on her to solve all their financial problems will be enormous.
5   Never trust her completely.
6   Remember the old adage: "Married men live longer than single men, but married men are a lot more willing to die."

CHAPTER 11

The *Fa-lung* inVestor

"The only way to make a small fortune in Pattaya is to start with a large one!"

Thailand is so wonderful, isn't it? The climate, the food, the smiling people, the lifestyle? And Pattaya? Well, it is just the icing on the cake. Wouldn't it be nice to settle down here and live out the rest of your life in this paradise on earth? You could retire here without too much problem but it would be even better to start your own business and make enough money to keep you in a lifestyle to which you would love to be accustomed. It would also give you something to do in your twilight years. Right?

Maybe, but this chapter is not about showing you how to set up a business in Thailand. That exercise would require several reams of paper plus more knowledge than I could ever hope to attain in my lifetime. Many bar owners and business people have imparted some advice and tips that should be passed on to anyone considering a business adventure. The list is just the tip of the iceberg.

Excluding those foreigners who work for large established companies or those on salaries from foreign companies, there are three types of *fa-lung* businessmen in Pattaya.

143

Type 1: The very small percentage of the working (legally or otherwise) expat population who actually do make money. Not a lot of money, mind you, but enough to make their lives comfortable. These guys will never become millionaires in dollar terms and are easily recognizable by their flat foreheads. This has been caused by continually beating their heads against Thai brick walls. They have thrown away their economics and business management books and theories that work perfectly well in the real world. They have recognized the 'Thai Factors' in their business dealings and decisions and are resolved to playing the Thai game.

Type 2: The ones who don't make much money from their business but simply survive. They invariably have a pension or other source of income coming in from their own country and most of their disposable income is consumed by alcohol. These guys may or may not recognize the 'Thai Factors' just as they may or may not recognize their own mother. They, consciously or unconsciously, play the Thai game and make up about one quarter of Thailand's foreign businessmen.

Type 3: The vast majority of the businessmen who come to Thailand, invest in, start up or buy a business venture that devours all their cash reserves within six months. These guys try to run the business the way they would run it in their own country or worse still, let someone else run it while they are out cavorting and drinking what they believe to be the profits. They are like a mouse on a treadmill, expending a lot of energy but getting absolutely nowhere. Hence, they only last as long as their own money does and walk (or run) away scratching their heads wondering where it all went. They failed to take into account the 'Thai factors'.

Dave invested some 50,000 baht in his girlfriend's prawn farm. One day, while drinking with a group of friends, he produced a plate containing some large yet unspectacular prawns for the group.

"Is this a sample of your prawn harvest?" one of the friends asked.
"What sample?" Dave replied sheepishly. "This is it – the entire harvest!"
It seems that Dave had failed to take into account the Thai factors when it came to his business venture. After allowing for all the stock that was stolen from the unguarded pond, all the ones eaten by his girlfriend's family, all of those sold prematurely by these same in-laws and all the prawns that simply died of neglect, his part of the deal amounted to about 500 grams.
"Dave, this is the first time in my life that I've eaten prawns that cost 100,000 baht per kilo."
Dave, of course, failed to see the funny side of it.

So, what are these 'Thai Factors'? They are a conglomeration of frustrations that, like ants at a picnic table, come out of nowhere, annoy the living hell out of you, devour all they can and refuse to go away until you have nothing left. At that point, they leave just as quickly and as stealthily as they arrived.

Thai factors include: people not turning up for appointments; not being able to obtain the simplest piece of information; delays in work for no apparent reason; sudden price rises above the original quote for the job; un-notified law changes; staff not turning up for work; agents running away with deposits; miles of red tape and regulations; shoddy workmanship etc. The list goes on.

Just like the ants, there is no singular defense against them. There is no global weapon or inoculation against them. As soon as you defeat one, another will pop up out of nowhere to take its place. It is a war of attrition. He who is the strongest and can last the longest, wins.

For anyone almost thinking about wishing to investigate the possibility of perhaps conducting a business in Thailand, what follows is a brief summary of some of the advice I received from *fa-lung* who have-been-there-done-that.

1   Never rush into any business deal no matter how good it may sound. Especially if it sounds like a great deal. Never pay any money up front. Take a lot of time to gather all the information before investing one *baht* in any business. Make a list of all the possible scams and ways that you could be cheated out of your money. Once you have finished your list, remind yourself that the person, whether Thai or *fa-lung*, proposing the deal to you has probably also thought of them – and then some. Nothing is beyond the realms of possibility.

2   As a foreigner, you should not attempt to do it on your own. You need to have an intelligent Thai partner who you can trust. Finding the right partner is extremely difficult but your business may fail without him or her. The exact partnership arrangement can be worked out between yourselves. Remember though, your Thai partner will have to be the front man or woman in the business. You can have all the great ideas and innovations you like but you need the Thai National to make them legal, to put them into effect and hopefully make them work.

3   Apart from your Thai business partner above, the less people involved in the Management side of the business the better. Try to avoid being talked into hiring or using any friends or relatives of your girlfriend or partner. Never let your Thai wife or girlfriend convince you to use a member of her family as your consultant. "Brother me big lawyer Bangkok. He do for free." He may in fact be a good lawyer and he may also offer his services for free (I doubt it), but who's interests do you think he will be looking after? If you answered, "Mine, because I am his client," go straight to the bottom of the class. Better still, go directly to Don Muang airport, do not pass *go-hok* and don't forget the 500 *baht* departure tax.

4   Do not count on any help from Thais, apart from your business partner, to make your venture a success. It is a sad fact that most of them do not want you to succeed. They want you to fail and the sooner the better. Take, for example, operating a bar. The

investor buys the business and pays out a lot of non-refundable money, including Key Money. He may also renovate and upgrade the premises. If the enterprise goes to the wall within a few months, most foreign investors simply walk away. The owner of the premises or the person who 'owns' the lease is then free to sell it again to someone else. He knows and understands that "there is a sucker born every minute." The monthly rent he receives from a working bar is nothing compared to the money he can make by selling it over and over again.

5   Never part with one *baht* or sign any document before attaining the services of a lawyer. I know of one poor fellow who paid over a lot of cash to buy a boat only to discover later that the ownership transfer document he signed was for a car, not a boat. He had purchased a very expensive, early model, petrol-guzzling, smoke-belching, rust-bucket of a car and had no way out because he had signed a legal document stating, in effect, that he was happy with the deal.

If you don't know a good lawyer, ask every expat you meet if they can recommend one to you. Attend expat association meetings. Eventually one name will keep recurring, in which case you can be reasonably sure that he or she has at least done the right thing by some expats in the past.

6   Walk, no RUN away from any deal where the other party suggests that you need not go through a lawyer because it will only cost extra money. The same goes if the other party offers the services of his or her own lawyer at a discount price.

7   Have all documents translated into English by an independent source. Better still, obtain two separate translations and compare them to ensure that the meaning is the same.

8   If, at any time during negotiations, you think you smell a rat, then be sure that there is the biggest mother of a rodent just sitting there waiting to pick you clean.

9   Whenever large amounts of money are transferred or withdrawn, insist that all partners be present at the bank. On more than one occasion in the past, the person who received the *fa-lung's* money also walked off with it.

10   Further on this point, as far as practicable, avoid using agents or intermediaries whenever money is concerned. As happens in many places throughout the world, agents have been known to pocket the money for themselves. When the real owner discovers that he has not been paid, the agent is nowhere to be found and receipt or no receipt, the buyer may be required to pay the money again.

11   Don't let emotion enter into any decision-making. Use your head at all times and distance it completely from your heart. If your ladylove nags you or threatens to leave you if you don't buy this or invest in that, then bid her farewell. It is far better to wave her goodbye than to chance waving goodbye to your money. If the latter did happen, you can be certain that she would follow soon after anyway. Console yourself with the fact that, given the option of losing the love of your life or your life savings, you have lost the one that is the most easily replaced.

12   If you are considering purchasing property, any property, whether it be a condo, shop, bar, house or vacant land, make sure you first find out who actually owns it. This could be difficult as title searches are not as straightforward as they are in the West. The property could be owned by one person, a company, a family or several people. There are also fake or forged titles around. One of the most costly scams involving an unwary *fa-lung* is to sell him property that is not owned or fully owned by the seller. The seller pockets the money and when the real owner or other owner finds out, the authorities can evict the *fa-lung*. Any piece of paper or so-called legal document that the foreigner holds as proof of purchase is not worth the paper it is written on. Sometimes, the real owner or other owners are involved in the scam and the one property can be 'sold' over and over again.

13   This is Thailand. Don't start whining when things don't go the way you planned. Don't go complaining that, "back home we would do it like this" or, "in my country it would work like this." You are not in 'your country' so you have to accept the way and the pace at which things are done here. If you can't do that, go home before your health suffers.

14   Follow the example of the Chinese. Ask a Chinese businessman how his business is going and he will complain that he is losing money every day. "Business no good. Only make enough money to eat rice." That is why Hong Kong, Singapore and Taiwan are poor impoverished places, because all Chinese-run businesses lose money. Learn the lesson from the Chinese. If your enterprise is successful and does make money, don't tell anyone!

15   There are strict rules regarding foreigners working in Thailand. You are not allowed to work without a work permit and these take a bit of effort and money to obtain. You will NOT get a work permit for running a bar. If you own a bar or restaurant and so much as put a glass in the sink, it could be construed as 'working' and you can be deported for it. (Now do you understand Point 14 above? Should you be seen as making a lot of money from your business, a phone call from a greedy friend or jealous competitor can get you into extreme trouble with the authorities.)

16   You must be prepared to keep constant control and sight on the daily operation of your business. Don't turn your back on it for a moment and continually check on the cash. Don't let too much cash end up in one person's hands, except yours, of course. Reconcile your financial dealings frequently and personally oversee all work. Don't go on too many 'holidays' and for most of the time, stay sober.

17   Do not listen to any Thai or expat who tells you they can help you with something because they have one or two powerful friends. "I know big Mafia" or "I am friends with the Chief of

Police." Many people exaggerate their sphere of influence in order to elevate their importance in the community. DO NOT rely on any of them to get you out of a jam and I don't care who they say they know or who they are related to. If you ever find yourself in trouble, the only thing that may get you out of it is money.

(Just an afterthought, but the Police Chiefs of Thailand seem to have an inordinate number of friends and relatives and why is it that everyone seems to know someone in the Mafia yet the police don't? Did I just answer my own question?)

18   NEVER tell your wife and/or business partner that you have a life insurance policy to provide for them or the business if something should happen to you. Never be worth more dead than alive because, in this part of the world, it can be arranged.

19   Finally, if your business partner also happens to be your girlfriend or wife, unless you have her prior permission, don't screw around. This is especially true if you are thinking about owning or managing a bar. Pattaya is full of temptations but it is a deceptively small place, gossip is the local pastime and YOU WILL GET CAUGHT! As well as probably ending your relationship, it could also end your business. Should there be a non-amicable parting of the ways, guess how much of the business you will end up with?

20   Always remember that this is Thailand. The Western-style legal system doesn't apply here, Western-style business ethics can not be found here and Western-style legal recourse in the case of dishonest business practice is unheard of here.

Does all that scare you? Good.

CHAPTER 12

Conclusion

*"Experience is something you don't get
until just after you need it."*

Well gentlemen, someone has just rung the bell so the class is over. There are other topics I could have covered, some I should have covered and more I would have liked to have covered but it is impossible to encompass all contingencies. Some, especially regarding legal matters or visa/immigration laws, I deliberately avoided because situations change too quickly. What is 'fact' today may be outdated tomorrow.

At the time of writing there were moves within the Thai Government to have places of entertainment close by midnight. I can just see tourists travelling thousands of kilometres and spending thousands of dollars to come to a country where they are forced to return to their hotel by midnight. If restrictive laws were implemented, the Thai tourism industry and therefore the Thai people would suffer and this book would become an historical document about a town which once thrived rather than a contemporary social commentary.

Fortunately, for the time being at least, backlash from the business community and people involved in the tourism industry forced the

151

government to have a rethink. We can only hope their well-intentioned but misguided plan has been filed in the 'too hard' basket indefinitely.

Until then, and while it lasts, there is no trick to enjoying or loving Pattaya or Thailand. That part is easy. I know a group of rabid golfers who came here for a seven-day golfing blowout but never touched a golf club or saw a fairway the entire time. Another guy extended his visa twice and changed his plane ticket six times because he just could not bear to leave.

The trick, therefore, is not to love it too much. To do this you must always remember that it is only a fantasy, a dream. It is a place where, as one wit noted, "some days you are the bug, some days you are the windshield." Keep your guard up, prepare for the unexpected and have the time of your life while you're doing it.

My love affair with the place began in 1998 and will end only if the dream does or when the first sods of earth fall against the lid of my coffin. For as complicated, illogical, incomprehensible and as downright irritating as it can be at times, one thing is sure and certain - life here is never dull.

The phrase "Money Number One" is the personification of Pattaya but whether you are a millionaire or a pauper, the fun is here to be shared by all. For visitors who have never been here before, I can only reiterate the words of the toilet-wall philosopher who wrote: "Don't worry. It only seems kinky the first time."

And I still hate the departure lounge at Don Muang Airport!